THE CENTURY COMPANION TO
THE WINES OF
SPAIN AND
PORTUGAL

CENTURY PUBLISHING

LONDON

Also in this series

The Century Companion to Bordeaux *Pamela Vandyke Price*
The Century Companion to Whiskies *Derek Cooper*
The Century Companion to Cognac and Other Brandies *James Long*

Series Editor Pamela Vandyke Price

First published in Great Britain in 1977 by
Pitman Publishing Limited
Revised edition published in 1983 by
Century Publishing Co Ltd
76 Old Compton Street, London W1V 5PA

ISBN 0 7126 0251 8

Reproduced, printed and bound in Great Britain by
Hazell Watson & Viney Limited,
Member of the BPCC Group,
Aylesbury, Bucks

Contents

SPAIN

1	**The Land**	3
2	**The History**	7
3	**What the Wines Are:**	13

Sherry 13

Montilla-Moriles 16

Other Flor-forming Wines 17

The Rioja 17

Catalonia 20

Navarra 21

Old Castile-León 21

Wine in Bulk 22

Green Wines 24

Dessert Wines 25

Sparkling Wines 26

4 **Control and Labelling** 27

5 **The Regions** 31

Visiting Wineries 34

Andalusia 35

The Rioja 45

Old Castile and León 53

Catalonia 55

Aragón and Navarra 62

Galicia 64

Extremadura 66

New Castile and the Levante 67

Balearics 69

Spirits, Aromatic Wines and Liqueurs 70

6 Regional Cooking 73

PORTUGAL

7 The Land and History 79

8 What the Wines Are: 85

Port 85

Madeira 88

Vinhos Verdes 88

Dão 90

Demarcated Wines of the Centre 92

Bairrada 92

Undemarcated Wines 93

9 Control and Labelling 95

10 The Regions: 98

Organising a Tour 98

Suggested Itinerary 100

Wines of the Centre 100

Oporto 103

Vinhos Verdes 107

The Upper Douro 110

Dão 114

Bairrada 116

Madeira 116

Spirits and Aromatic Wines 117

11 Regional Cooking 119

APPENDICES

1 Wine Tasting – by Pamela Vandyke Price 121

2 Glossary of Wine Terms 129

3 Further Reading 131

4 Wine Regulations 132

Index 135

Maps

The wine-growing areas of the Iberian Peninsula 6

Spain 32

The Rioja 46

Catalonia 56

Portugal 99

PART ONE

SPAIN

1

The Land

Spain has more land under vines than any other country in Europe, yet her production of wine is only about a third that of either Italy or France. That most percipient observer of the *cosas de España*, the early nineteenth-century traveller Richard Ford, wrote that 'The wines of Spain, under a latitude where a fine season is a certainty, might rival those of France, and still more those of the Rhine, where a good vintage is the exception, not the rule. Their varieties are infinite, since few districts, unless those that are very elevated, are without their local produce, the names, colours, and flavours of which are equally numerous and varied.'

Ford put down the discrepancy to the 'unscientific, careless manner' in which much of the wine was made, a phrase echoed today by Hugh Johnson when he speaks of 'the slightly desultory nature of a great deal of Spain's wine industry'. With the intervention of the highly organised sherry concerns and the banks in the production of better quality table wines and the spread of scientifically organised co-operatives, all this is undergoing a sea-change; but the quality and quantity of the wine will always be subject to the fundamental considerations of soil and climate.

The Iberian Peninsula is the most mountainous region in Europe apart from Switzerland, and has been likened to an inverted soup plate, the central area consisting of a high, barren plateau (Madrid, near the centre, is 668 m high), bitingly cold in winter and scorchingly hot in summer. The rim of the dish corresponds to fertile coastal fringe, wide enough around Valencia and Cartagena, extending inland up the Guadalquivir basin into Andalusia, and of very considerable extent in central and southern Portugal. A further glance at the map reveals a series of great mountain massifs with spurs running down to the sea. It is almost impossible to travel towards the coast in any direction from Madrid without crossing a mountain barrier; and Portugal is screened by a range of mountains running from north to south along the frontier, penetrated only by the valleys of the Guadiana and Tagus in the south and centre, and those of the Duero (Douro) and Miño (Minho) in the north.

For good reason the country's rulers were called 'King of the Spains' rather than 'King of Spain'; and in terms of history, climate and geography Spain is not one country but many. It is difficult to imagine greater extremes than the lush pastures of the Basque country; the endless grey-green olive groves of Jaén; the fertile, semi-tropical *huertas* or market gardens of Valencia, with their crops of oranges, lemons, sugar cane and rice; the vast wheat fields and vineyards of La Mancha; or the parched scrubland of the Extremadura with its roving flocks of sheep and pigs.

It is therefore impossible to generalise about Spanish wines except on a regional basis. They are as various as the country itself; and this variety stems from extremes of soil and climate and methods of cultivation and vinification appropriate to the local conditions.

Sherry is a wine apart, an artefact, which in the first place owes its entirely individual character to the chalky *albariza* soils and the clays and sands of the southern tip of the Peninsula, and to the relentless Andalusian sun. In terms of soil and climate the regions to the west towards Portugal, and to the north towards Córdoba, are somewhat similar; and the rainfall is so low that the vines are trained and pruned low and banked to catch what rain there is, which is retained in the chalk and clays of the subsoil during the long hot summer.

The vine is notoriously a plant which thrives on barren soil, and it is significant that the most famous wine town of the central plateau, supplying vast amounts of everyday drinking wine to other parts of the country, is called Valdepeñas – or *Val de Peñas*, meaning the 'valley of stones'. The great rolling expanses of La Mancha, a vivid green in the spring and burnished copper in autumn, are arid – again with a chalky subsoil which absorbs and retains the winter rain.

Further to the east, along the broad coastal plain of the Levante, the soil is rich and alluvial and ideally suited to the cultivation of semi-tropical crops and spring vegetables – witness the endless convoys of heavy trucks along the great coastal highway, bound for the markets of France. The best of the grapes is the sweet dessert Moscatel, also used for making raisins, which demands different conditions from those suitable for fine wines. That Victorian pioneer of scientific oenology, Cyrus Redding, saw a great future for the wines of the Levante and predicted that 'Southward of France geographically, Spain should, from its happier clime as a vine-growing country, precede it in the excellence of its wine . . .' This was to overlook the fact that hot and unremitting sunshine produces excessive amounts of sugar in the fruit and coarse wines overstrong in alcohol.

All the southern regions of Spain – Andalusia, Levante, New Castile and the Extremadura – burn under the same blazing sun. In the cooler mountain areas behind Málaga and on the Valencian border, and in parts of the Extremadura towards

Portugal, where slate and clay predominate, careful husbandry produces wines of character; but it is the more temperate north of Spain which grows the country's best table wines.

Of all the wine districts, the best-known outside Jerez, the Rioja, most resembles the classical wine-producing areas abroad. Some 100 km long, it centres on the wide upland valley of the River Ebro, sheltered by low hills on either side. The subsoil is derived from sandstone, chalk and limestone, topped by alluvial deposits from the Ebro and its tributaries. The springs are mild and wet, the summers short and hot, and the autumns long and warm, so that picking does not start until mid-October. As in all the other regions of Spain except Galicia the vines are grown *a la castellana* – pruned low and unsupported by the wires common in Bordeaux. Spain, although rather later than France, suffered from the ravages of that aphid pest of the vine, *phylloxera*, towards the end of the nineteenth and at the beginning of the twentieth century; and it is normal practice in the Rioja, as elsewhere, to graft cuttings from the native varieties of *Vitis vinifera* on to the root stocks of the American *Vitis riparia* or *Vitis rupestris*, or the *Berlandieri* and its hybrids, which are resistant to the insect. The grapes grown in the cooler and higher sub-regions to the west of the area receive less sunshine than those from the hotter and drier Rioja Baja to the east; for this reason they contain less sugar and produce more delicate wines with less alcohol. There are also significant differences in the wines made from grapes grown on slopes with a southern or northern aspect.

The west and mountainous north coast of Spain produces excellent cider, but very little wine; and disregarding smaller regions like Navarra, Cariñena, Ribera del Duero, Rueda, Toro and Léon, the other important wine-producing areas are those of Catalonia and Galicia.

A great deal of good wine is made in Catalonia, where climatic conditions are temperate and favourable. The soils vary from the granitic of Alella, north of Barcelona, to the limestone of Penedès and the decayed lava and ferruginous slate of Priorato in the mountainous area to the south.

Galicia in the far north-west is an area apart. The wet climate and granitic soil have given rise to methods of viticulture very similar to those employed in northern Portugal for making *vinhos verdes* ('green wines'). As in Portugal, the vines are trained high, often on wires strung between granite pillars, so as to keep the grapes clear of the wet soil and free from mildew and parasitic rot and also to afford maximum exposure to sunlight. Even so, it is customary for the wines to undergo a secondary so-called malo-lactic fermentation to eliminate excess acid from grapes that are not fully ripened.

If it is impossible to describe the numerous and variegated

wine-growing regions of Spain with the precision of a neat and compact area like Bordeaux or Burgundy, it is equally difficult to suggest an itinerary. To obtain a full picture one must travel the length and breadth of Spain, a journey involving some 15,000 kilometres and six weeks on the road. The more sensible scheme is to visit one or two of the main areas at a time. Barcelona is a good starting point for Catalonia, Navarra and the Rioja; Madrid or Valencia for La Mancha and the Levante; and Seville for Andalusia and the sherry country. Galicia involves a trip on its own – pleasant enough if combined with visits to Santiago de Compostela and its sandy Atlantic coves.

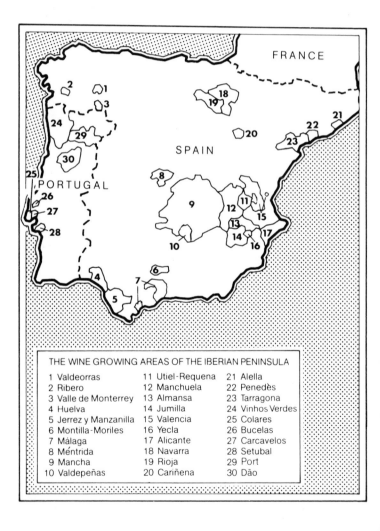

THE WINE GROWING AREAS OF THE IBERIAN PENINSULA

1 Valdeorras	11 Utiel-Requena	21 Alella
2 Ribero	12 Manchuela	22 Penedès
3 Valle de Monterrey	13 Almansa	23 Tarragona
4 Huelva	14 Jumilla	24 Vinhos Verdes
5 Jerrez y Manzanilla	15 Valencia	25 Colares
6 Montilla-Moriles	16 Yecla	26 Bucelas
7 Málaga	17 Alicante	27 Carcavelos
8 Méntrida	18 Navarra	28 Setubal
9 Mancha	19 Rioja	29 Port
10 Valdepeñas	20 Cariñena	30 Dão

2

The History

Whether the vine was a native of the Iberian Peninsula or was brought there from the East during the migrations of the prehistoric period is an open question. After men first learned about fermentation they improved on the wild grape vines by processes of cultivation and selection. When the Phoenicians and the Greeks formed settlements along the Mediterranean coast they instituted new methods of viticulture; and the stone and earthenware vats employed by the Phoenicians in Cyprus bear a strong resemblance to those still in use in country districts of Aragón.

The Carthaginians made more determined inroads and, by attempting to use the country as a base for the conquest of Italy, attracted the opposition of Rome. It was as a result of the counter-offensive against Hannibal during the Second Punic War, when, after capturing Saguntum in 219 BC, he crossed into Italy via the passes of the eastern Pyrenees and the Alps, that the Romans arrived in force to cut him off from his bases in Hispania. Thereafter, the Romans occupied the whole region; but it took two centuries of hard guerrilla fighting before the province was securely incorporated in the Empire.

By the time of Augustus (63 BC to AD 14) great advances had been made in agriculture and in viticulture in particular. The great discovery of *amphorae* at Monte Testaccio near Rome, many of them bearing their seals of origin, testifies to the large importation of wine from the Peninsula. Indeed, by the beginning of the first century AD it was found necessary to protect the Italian growers by enforcing strict limitations on the planting of new vines in the Hispanic provinces. In Roman times the wine was fermented and kept in large earthenware jars called *orcae*; and this tradition still persists in Montilla and La Mancha.

There are numerous references to Spanish wines in Latin literature. The sweet wines of Málaga were a great favourite: the Spanish-born Columella, writing in the first century AD, treats of them in Book IV of his *De Re Rustica* and in Book III of the *Agricultura*, while Pliny, Democritus and Virgil also praised them. Catalonia was another important centre of production, and under the shadow of the viaduct near Montserrat there exists a vineyard almost certainly planted in Roman times. As the legions fanned out they brought with them a healthy thirst, and as far afield as Galicia there is a legend that the *clarete* of Amandi was served to the Emperor Augustus to wash down his spiced lamprey.

A Roman amphora

With the decline of the Roman Empire, the country was overrun during the fourth and fifth centuries AD by Gothic tribes from northern Europe, themselves supplanted by the Moors from North Africa, who dominated the southern half of the country for some five centuries after the first landings in 711. In deference to the Koran's prohibition, wine was usually made and sold by the Christians; but evidence enough as to its wide enjoyment and consumption, even by the emirs and caliphs, is the many poems in its praise. So al-Mu'tamid (1040–95), the poet king of Seville, could write a eulogy of the vine or Ibn Mujbar of Murcia (d. 1191) a poem, which with great sophistication condemns the practice of serving wine in coloured glasses:

> I certainly intend
> Complaining to my friend
> About this glass, alack
> Garmented all in black.
>
> I set therein to shine
> The sunlight of the wine;
> The sun is sinking thence
> To darkness most intense.

The beaker, coloured so,
Denies the liquor's glow,
As envious hearts disown
The favours they have known.

translated by A. J. Arberry
Moorish Poetry, Cambridge, 1953

In *Gods, Men and Wine* (Wine and Food Society and Michael Joseph, 1966), William Younger lists the areas of mediaeval Spain from which wines were exported abroad. They include Alicante, Garnarde (Granada), Málaga, Lepe (near the modern Huelva), Ryvere and Torrentyne (possibly the modern Rioja, but more probably the Ebro valley generally) and Xérès (sherry). The mediaeval practice of viticulture has been particularly well-documented in Catalonia, which differed from Spain as a whole. In the south of the country the *latifundia* or great estates of the Roman-Gothic nobility persisted in modified form well into modern times, but the Counts of Barcelona and the Kings of Aragon-Catalonia, notably James the Conqueror (1213–76), pursued a healthy policy of settling the farmers on their own land. From the ninth century onwards it became the custom for a proprietor to lease land to a farmer on condition that he should plant it with vines, first sharing the produce and later the vineyard itself. The *Rabassa Morta*, as this practice was known, expired only on the death of the first-planted vines; and as they were long-lived in the pre-*phylloxera* era, it was a binding engagement of long duration. The bodegas in Catalonia were commonly known as *sacrarios*; and this originated from the practice of locating them in the *sacraria*, or sanctified burial area around a church, where they were safe from the depredations of thieves.

Wine-growing in Spain received a new stimulus with the discovery and conquest of America and an insatiable demand for home-grown wines from the Conquistadors. From this point the history of the two most important areas, Jerez and the Rioja, deserves more detailed consideration.

Jerez has been famous for its wines since Roman times, and it is said that when Martial commends 'Caeretana' he is in fact referring to sherry. If one cannot go all the way with Richard Ford in his judgment that 'Sherry is a foreign wine, and made and drunk by foreigners', it is nevertheless true that the activity of foreign merchants both in buying and making sherry contributed a great deal to its present perfection. There are records of the wine being exported to England as early as 1340 during the reign of Edward III, and in the *Pardoner's Tale* Chaucer (who was a vintner's son) celebrates the strength of the wine from nearby Lepe:

Now keep ye from the white and from the red,
And namely from the white wine of Lepe,
That is to sell in Fish Street or in Chepe.
This wine of Spain creepeth subtilly
In other wines, growing fast by,
Of which there riseth such fumositee,
That when a man hath drunken draughtes three,
And weneth that he be at home in Chepe,
He is in Spain, right at the town of Lepe,
Not at the Rochelle, nor at Bordeaux town.

After the Catholic Monarchs brought the reconquest of the country from the Moors to a triumphant conclusion in 1492 by the capture of Granada, one of their first steps in what had become a crusade for Catholicism, was to expel the Jews. In Jerez, the place of the Jewish merchants was taken by Genoese, Bretons and the English, who largely cornered the market in wines. In spite of political differences during the Tudor period, the English community grew; and the only lasting result of Sir Francis Drake's raid on Cadiz in 1587 and his seizure of 2,900 pipes of wine was to clinch its popularity in England.

The wine achieved fame under its old name of sack (probably from the Spanish *sacar*, to 'export'); and, of numerous references to it in the literature of the time, Prince Hal's complaint to Falstaff, 'O monstrous! but one half-pennyworth of bread to this intolerable deal of sack', is but the best-known. The wine was in fact a great deal sweeter than a modern sherry; and it is on record that even a century later in 1662 Samuel Pepys mixed two butts of sherry ('the first great quantity of wine I ever bought') with four gallons of Málaga.

After a temporary decline in popularity during the earlier part of the eighteenth century, attributable in part to the Methuen Treaty of 1703, which gave preference to Portuguese wines in the English market, the trade picked up in the last decades of the century and there was a tremendous expansion after the Peninsular War and during the early 1800s. It was from this era that the great sherry firms of today took shape, often by the amalgamation of smaller firms. Many resulted from the initiative of English, Scots and Irish merchants who had either settled in the area, like the Gordon family, or Sir James Duff, British consul in Cadiz during the latter half of the eighteenth century, or those who left the desks of their shipping businesses in London to take over on the spot. Their memory is enshrined in the household names of today: Duff Gordon, Osborne, Garvey, Gonzalez Byass, Sandeman, and Williams and Humbert. One large house, that of Pedro Domecq, also associated with the father of the poet John Ruskin, was founded by an Irishman, Patrick Murphy, who arrived in Spain at some time prior to 1730, but owes its present pre-eminence to the energy of a Frenchman, the great Pedro Domecq Lembeye.

Sherry suffered something of an eclipse at the turn of the nineteenth century, when late Victorian taste was for the now unfashionable wines of Málaga and the almost forgotten Tarragona – an inferior imitation of port – but has long since regained its pre-eminence. Though in recent years sales of sherry, in common with those of other fortified wines, have declined, Britain is still the largest consumer, followed by Holland.

The history of wine-growing in the Rioja also dates back to the Romans, if not before – there were legions stationed at Cenicero (the word means an 'ash tray' and the village took its name from the Roman burial ground) and Gimileo near Ollauri, both important wine centres. The Rioja was known as '*Veled Assikia*' in Moorish times and was one of the first regions to be reconquered by the Christians. By 1592, when, like Jerez, it was devoted to slaking the thirst of the Conquistadors, King Philip II commented on the unprecedented abundance of vineyards in the area, and expansion continued during the seventeenth century with detriment to the quality of the wine.

It was perhaps symptomatic of the era of 'enlightened despotism' of Charles III that by 1790 a 'Royal Society of the Harvesters of the Rioja' had been founded to improve viticulture and viniculture and also to expand markets. The Society planned a new road from Logroño to Haro to 'establish a comfortable [means of] communication through the lands of Castile and so to facilitate our exports of abundant and precious fruits and our imports of scarce products either from European ports or from our Americas.' Work was held up by the outbreak of the Peninsular War and the road was not finally completed until 1831, but in the meantime the Society had given the growers the wise advice that 'the export of your most abundant crops will not become a reality unless the wines again acquire the superior quality which they must have in our province . . .' Many Riojan wine-makers took these counsels to heart and travelled to France to study in Bordeaux and Burgundy. When *phylloxera* first attacked the Bordeaux vineyards, supplies were made good from the Rioja and a number of French viticulturalists settled in the region. Their expertise rubbed off, and one of the results was the adoption of the 225-litre oaken Bordeaux *barrique*, universally used for maturing Rioja wines today. By the late 1800s the standard type of Rioja table wine, light and pleasant, had been firmly established.

Other regions of Spain better-known for quantity than quality have also gained a reputation for their wines outside Spain. Valdepeñas, which Ford regarded as the best of Spanish table wines, was also the favourite of the Emperor Charles V and was carted across Europe on mule-back during his campaigns in the Low Countries; Málaga was the preferred wine both of the ill-fated Tamburlaine and of Catherine the Great of Russia; and at one time the strong red wines of Navarra were also much fancied in Russia.

Perhaps strangest of all was the dark, full-bodied and alcoholic wine of Benicarló in the Levante – Ford's 'black strap' of ill repute – which in the early years of the nineteenth century was exported in large amounts to France to 'fret' (or boost) the delicate growth of Bordeaux for English palates blunted by the inordinate consumption of port.

During the last decade there have been sweeping changes in the Spanish wine industry. In preparation for Spain's impending entry into the Common Market, numerous additional regions have been demarcated; and some of them, such as Rueda and León (as yet undemarcated), are exporting wine on a large scale. One of the achievements of the Franquist regime was to create a new middle class with a taste for better quality bottled wine and the means to indulge it. Nowhere has expansion been more rapid than in the Rioja, where the Spanish banks, the large sherry companies and international wine and spirit concerns, such as Pepsi-Cola, Seagram and the British IDV (International Distillers & Vintners) have constructed huge new bodegas. Since 1970, exports of Rioja to Britain alone have risen from an annual 180,000 litres to some 2,115,000.

Increased emphasis on better quality has been matched by advances in technology. In the co-operatives, which make so much of the wine for everyday consumption, it is now not uncommon to find closed vats of the Algerian type; while more sophisticated wineries are increasingly using stainless steel tanks, allowing for fermentation at lower temperatures and the retention of more of the aroma and flavour of the fruit. And Spanish wine-makers have looked outwards in other ways; much more importance, for example, is now being attached to vintage years and the ageing of the better wines in bottle.

The Mediterranean was the cradle of wine-making in Europe; but in the past, high summer temperatures have militated against the making of fine wines. Modern technology and improved methods of vinification are steadily altering the balance as between the classical wine-growing areas of the north and those of the south, with their more prolific, but less delicate growths.

3

What the Wines Are

Some indication has already been given of the geographical, geological and climatic extremes. More than a hundred different grape varieties are grown; fermentation may be carried out in wooden casks or vats, earthenware jars of all sizes, stone cisterns, cement deposits or stainless steel tanks, and the wines may be matured in oak or chestnut or even in glass *bombonas*, with or without access to the atmosphere. All these factors influence the taste and other characteristics of the end product, which ranges from apéritif wines to white, rosé and red table wines, 'green wines', dessert wines and sparkling wines, in addition to a wide variety of brandies, spirits, vermouths and liqueurs.

Sherry

Spain, like Portugal, is a country first and foremost famous for one wine, and even if its table wines are underrated and little known, sherry is a household word. Of all preliminaries to a meal, a glass of dry sherry is perhaps the best, since it stimulates rather than blunts the palate. Oddly enough, the problem of what to drink as an apéritif is at its most acute at a provincial bar in that most sophisticated of wine countries, France. One is confronted by an array of bottles, whose contents are as startlingly coloured as they are violent or sugary, and it is sometimes impossible to obtain even a glass of luke-warm Noilly Prat, let alone the delicious cold Chambéry. It is symptomatic that France is the largest importer of cheap port – usually drunk *before* and not after a meal – and even the drier white ports, pleasant as some of them are, cannot seriously challenge sherry as an apéritif. A sugary drink, with its high calorie content and penetrating taste, is of course the worst possible preliminary either to eating or to drinking wines. The French, possibly because of a historical antagonism, have never taken to sherry, and it must be admitted that it is perhaps at its best when drunk in the colder countries of northern Europe, where it has always been a favourite. In Spain itself, Spanish brandy, sometimes drunk with ice and soda, is vastly more popular. The present vogue for Scotch whisky in France, as elsewhere in Europe, is entirely understandable, since drunk with water it is a milder, drier and more delicate preliminary than most of its sticky competitors.

Most wines that grow a *flor* and are fermented in contact with air possess a generic 'sherry flavour', and the great sherry boom of the nineteenth century led to the production of wine by analogous methods in a variety of countries, notably South Africa, Australia, California and Cyprus. Some of the earlier imitations were positively unpleasant, and even today few of the wines possess the delicacy of the best *finos* from Jerez itself or the astonishing fragrance and bouquet of other fine Spanish sherries, although I am informed that the best of the South African sherries, unfortunately not shipped, are excellent wines in their own right. The best of the Spanish wines have never been surpassed, and in view of rising costs are excellent value, though some of the inexpensive wine now being shipped is on more of a par with its foreign competitors. In an attempt to hold down prices in the shops, the size of the standard 75 cl bottle has sometimes been reduced, a practice now being extended to table wines and to be deplored unless the contents are clearly marked.

It is impossible to describe the intrinsic taste of sherry, but it arises from fermenting the appropriate type of grape with free access to the atmosphere. Of the different vines, the most important is the Palomino, which grows best on the *albariza* soil. Although the Pedro Ximénez can be used for making dry wines and is habitually used for this purpose in the neighbouring region of Montilla-Moriles, its principal use in Jerez is for making sweet dessert sherries. It is sometimes said that the grape first grew in the Canary Islands and was later taken to the Rhine, whence it was brought to Spain in the sixteenth century by one Peter (in Spanish, Pedro) Siemens, a soldier of the Emperor Charles V – but the story is almost certainly apocryphal. A third important grape is the Moscatel, used in preparing sweet wines to blend with the rich dessert sherries made for export.

In normal circumstances fermentation in the presence of air would result in oxidation of the wine and its conversion to vinegar, were it not that the new wine or must has the property of growing a thick protective layer of yeasts, known as a '*flor*' (or 'flower') on the surface. Consistency in the end product is obtained by using a *solera*, in which younger wines are used for the progressive replenishment of butts of the more mature wines, as it is drawn off for further blending, fortification and shipping.

No two butts of young wine develop in quite the same way, and at an early stage in its development the wine is earmarked for one of three basic types.

Fino, of 15° to 18° alcoholic strength (15° implies 15 per cent by volume of alcohol), is the palest, lightest and most delicate of sherries. Like other sherries, it is completely dry in its natural state, but is often slightly sweetened for the British market and different brands vary considerably in this respect. When left to mature it grows steadily more intense in flavour, finally developing into an *amontillado* of 16° to 18° strength, deeper in colour and possessing its own distinctive bouquet and 'nutty' flavour.

Palo Cortado, of some 17.5° to 23° strength, is now something of a rarity and little of it is shipped. It is sometimes classed as a style of *oloroso*, but is made in its own special *solera* and in its deep and fragrant bouquet more resembles an *amontillado*. Somewhat darker than an *amontillado*, it is classified as *dos*, *tres* or *cuatro cortados* according to age. The genuine article is always expensive, and it should be bought only from a shipper of high standing.

Oloroso, which does not grow a *flor*, is the darkest and most obviously fragrant of sherries. Through a somewhat complex chemistry it may achieve strengths as high as 24°, and is again naturally dry, but since *olorosos* are frequently used for dessert sherries, they are often blended with a sweet *mistela* made by adding alcohol to musts of the Pedro Ximénez grape to arrest fermentation before the fruit sugars are consumed. The bulk of sherry drunk in the United Kingdom, though not in Spain, is sweet, and a great variety of wines of this type are elaborated specifically for export; it is in fact much easier to produce a standard brand, since the sweetness to some extent blurs the bouquet and flavour of the straight *solera* wine. These sweetened *olorosos* are sometimes, appropriately enough, called *amorosos* ('loving'), but are most often known as cream sherries. The forerunner and most famous is Harvey's Bristol Cream, at one time blended in Bristol itself, but more recently, since the firm acquired vineyards and bodegas in Jerez, blended on the spot with Pedro Ximénez and other sweetening and colouring wines. The best dessert *olorosos* from other firms like Sandemans, Williams and Humbert, Pedro Domecq and Gonzalez Byass and Avery's of Bristol, are of similar high quality.

Manzanilla is not made in Jerez, but in the small town of Sanlúcar de Barrameda on the Guadalquivir estuary. Though *manzanilla* is made from the same grapes, they are picked earlier and there are differences in its elaboration, so that it stands rather apart from the other sherries. It exists in various styles, but the word normally refers to an extremely dry *fino* with a penetrating aromatic fragrance, slightly less strong in alcohol than the *finos* from Jerez. Its *aficionados* claim to detect in it the salty tang of its native sea breezes.

Whatever its basic type, all sherry from the *solera* except the most expensive will normally undergo further blending, with the admixture of *mistela*, and *vino de color* (colouring wine) in the case of the dessert varieties, before reaching the market.

It is sometimes thought that sherry will keep indefinitely; but this is not wholly true. *Finos* and light *amontillados* should ideally be drunk within three months of bottling; once the bottle has been opened, they become noticeably less delicate after a few days. Dry *olorosos* keep well for several years; and dessert sherries improve with bottle age, as their sugar is slowly consumed. Dry *finos* should be drunk chilled and dessert sherries at room temperature.

Montilla-Moriles

The wines of Montilla-Moriles, from the district south of Córdoba, are so similar in style to sherry that before the region was demarcated most of its wine went to Jerez for blending, and a great deal of Montilla shipped abroad was sold under the name of its more famous relation. There are nevertheless significant differences. The most important grape of the region, the Pedro Ximénez, is not sun-dried as in Jerez to boost its sugar content, but picked and immediately fermented to completion; fermentation takes place not in oak butts, but in large earthenware containers called *tinajas*, and the wine is never fortified. The musts grow a *flor* and are therefore matured in wood in a *solera*, as in Jerez. The wine emerges as a *fino*, *amontillado*, *palo cortado* or *oloroso*, but when the Spaniard orders Montilla, he expects – and is unquestioningly given – the *fino*, a pale, dry wine with a greenish tint, containing some 14° to 17.5° of alcohol, fragrant and light on the palate. Montilla may be drunk as an apéritif, or, as it frequently is in Córdoba, chilled and throughout a meal, when it forms an excellent accompaniment to shellfish or highly spiced *tapas*. The Jerezanos drink *fino* sherry in the same way – the proprietor of one of the bodegas once told me that he drank nothing else with his food. And there is nothing particularly surprising about this, since *finos* for domestic consumption do not undergo a second fortification and the Spaniards are habituated to many very ordinary table wines containing as much alcohol as a *fino* sherry or montilla.

The word *tapa* means a cover, and it is sometimes said that its colloquial usage as an appetiser provided with a glass of wine in a bar originated from the practice of covering the glass. A few almonds, olives, prawns or a cube of *tortilla* (Spanish omelette) were formerly served with the compliments of the house, but the custom is unfortunately dying out. *Tapas*, however, are still very popular. From the dishes ranged along the top of the counter you may choose from things as substantial as crisp-fried rings of inkfish, Russian salad, stuffed peppers, mussels or marinated fish, but the *raciones* (or portions), especially of the delicious *percebes* (a form of edible barnacle), are anything but cheap.

Other Flor-forming Wines

Without the intense fragrance of sherry, there are various beverage wines which grow a *flor* and, without being matured in a *solera*, partake of its generic flavour. Some of them in fact contain as much or more alcohol as a *fino* sherry in a land where, thanks to the beating sun and high sugar content of the grapes, it is not unusual for table wines to be of 16° strength or in some cases to approach 18° – at which point the yeasts are killed and fermentation stops.

Much of the white wine from the Province of Huelva is of this nature, and the best of it has in fact been used to blend with the cheaper sherries. North of Huelva in the Extremadura, the village of Montánchez actually produces a *red* wine that grows a *flor* – but this is so unusual as to warrant more detailed comment later (see page 67). On the eastern fringe of the Extremadura the town of Cañamero near Guadalupe makes another such white wine with a reputation that has spread to Madrid. Better known and in much larger supply are the wines from west of Valladolid in Old Castile. Golden in colour, high in alcohol and sometimes lasting for as long as twenty-five years, they are firm on the palate and very pleasant to drink, with their pervading overtone of sherry.

The Rioja

Rioja is the best-known table wine from Spain. All Spanish restaurants of any repute list a selection, while abroad there are those for whom 'Rioja' is synonymous with Spanish wine in general. The region produces a great deal more red wine than white, and the choice reds are excellent wines by any yardstick. Beyond the peaks, such as the *reservas* from bodegas like Riscal, Murrieta, López de Heredia, La Rioja Alta and others, there is a sea of very drinkable wines.

Of the traditional white wines, Hugh Johnson once wrote that they are 'marvellously stony and up to Rhone wine standards'; and more recently the region has been making lighter and fresher whites, more in the style of those from the Loire or Alsace.

The main types are:

Clarete. Light red wines, made by limited contact with the skins during fermentation, bright in colour with a fragrant bouquet, often oaky, with good fruit and long finish.

Tinto. Full-bodied, dark in colour and of relatively high alcohol content; a typical *tinto* might contain some 12.5° (percentage by volume). Although the custom is dying out, the bodegas often used to label their wines Rioja-clarete and Rioja-Burgundy, and this is some guide to the style, though it is fruitless to press the comparison, because the French and Spanish wines are made from different grapes and by methods which are not the same.

Rosado. Rosé wines, either dry or sweet. The best are made by fermenting them like white wines, after allowing the must to take up a little colour and flavour from the skins. Cheaper rosés are made by mixing red and white wine.

Reservas. Wines of good vintage, aged for extended periods both in oak cask and bottle.

Blanco. White wines, either dry, semi-sweet or sweet. They range from the traditional type aged in cask, with their blend of oak and fruit in nose and flavour, to the light and fresh new-style whites made by 'cold fermentation' and not aged in oak.

The complete list of vine varieties grown in the Rioja runs to fourteen; but of these only seven are normally used for making fine Riojas.

Of the four grapes used for red Rioja, each makes its contribution to a balanced wine. The Garnacho is related to the French Grenache, but has long ago developed different characteristics and confers body and alcoholic strength. The other grapes are all thought to be native: the Tempranillo produces musts which on their own would be a little 'soft' because of insufficient acidity; the Graciano contributes freshness, flavour and aroma; the Mazuelo, rich in tannin, imparts long life, an important consideration with wines which are often matured for long periods in wood.

Prolonged ageing in wood is in fact one of the ways in which red Riojas have traditionally most differed from comparable French wines. Government regulations require that to qualify for Denominación de Origen 'Rioja', even the youngest of the wines *con crianza* ('with ageing'), both red and white, must be matured for not less than two years with a minimum of one in 225-litre oak *barricas*, traditionally made of wood from North America. Although there is a trend towards maturing Rioja for longer in bottle and less time in wood, the better wines, especially the *reservas*, may spend years in *barrica*, so acquiring the 'vanilla' nose and oaky flavour which has become their 'trademark'.

At the Marqués de Murrieta, for example, it has always been the custom to keep the wines in cask and to bottle them shortly before despatch – and few people would quarrel with the results after tasting the magnificent 1934 or 1942 'Castillo de Ygay' *reservas*. The danger, of course, of keeping wines for excessive periods in wood is that they may lose body, acquire too marked an oaky flavour and develop a degree of volatile acidity; and it is becoming increasingly common for the fine red wines to be aged for some two years in *barrica* with the balance in bottle.

White Riojas are made from three types of grape, often blended: the Viura, originally introduced from Aragón; the Malvasía, derived from the Greek grape of the same name, but grown in the Rioja, Castile and Navarra since times of antiquity; and the white Garnacho (or Garnacha). The wines are made in the usual fashion by separating skins and pips before fermentation, but now comprise two distinct types: those subsequently aged in oak, and others, lighter and fresher, fermented for periods of up to six weeks at temperatures as low as 16°C in stainless steel and not matured in oak. It would, however, be a pity if such thoroughly characterful wines as the 'Monopole' from CVNE, with its subtle blend of oak and fruit, or the beautiful old 'Tondonia' *reservas* from López de Heredia were eventually to disappear.

The Rioja differs from the classical French wine-growing areas in other important aspects. In contrast to the hundreds of châteaux and domaines in Bordeaux and Burgundy, there are only some fifty large bodegas entitled to export wines with the *denominación de origen*. Some have sizeable vineyards of their own, but not large enough to satisfy their substantial requirements of grapes. They therefore buy fruit from independent farmers or even co-operative-made wine for blending with their larger selling and less expensive wine. At a bodega like Murrieta or Riscal, control of such outside supplies is strict. At Murrieta the oenologist regularly inspects the vineyards of the select group of farmers from which the bodega buys. If he considers that the grapes are not up to standard, the bodega makes a token payment and arranges for them to be used elsewhere. It is here a point of pride that the grapes are picked and crushed on the same day, passing at once to the fermentation vats. Any grapes left for the following day are very carefully inspected and, if necessary, rejected.

In the Rioja as a whole there is a shortage of the grapes needed for the white wine, and Government regulations have at times been relaxed to allow the purchase of wine from other regions for blending.

Because of the usual predictability of the weather, the purchase of grapes from different parts of the region and the custom of blending small amounts of wine made in better years with the poorer vintages, the quality of the wine varies less from year to year than in France or Germany – hence the practice of labelling the younger and more moderately priced wines as bottled, say, in their third or fourth year (3° año, 4° año). This was never a very satisfactory form of labelling, since it gave no clue as to the vintage year or as to how long the wine had been in bottle. It is now being phased out, since EEC regulations require that quality wines shipped to Common Market countries be labelled with the year of vintage.

As regards vintages, perhaps the best of the last decade were 1970, 1973, 1976, 1980 and 1981, 1974 and 1975 were average years; a little good wine, like that from the Marqués de Riscal, was made in 1971; but 1979 was below average, and 1972 and 1977 uniformly disappointing. Outstanding earlier years, if you are fortunate enough to find a bottle, were 1952, 1955, 1964 and 1968.

Taking the Rioja as a whole and holding over the characteristics and style of the wines from individual bodegas for later consideration, those from the higher Rioja Alta and Rioja Alavesa are more delicate and less strong in alcohol than the wines from the Rioja Baja. As Sr. Antonio Larrea, former director of the Estación de Viticultura y Enología at Haro, has pointed out, this is because, as the Ebro loses height from west to east through the region, the ratio of sugar to other ingredients in the grape increases; and the sugar content is directly proportional to alcoholic strength after fermentation. Thus in the Rioja Alta the wines average between 11° and 12°, while in the Rioja Baja and in Navarra the strength increases to between 15° and 18°.

Catalonia

The most important of the wine-growing areas in Catalonia is the Penedès, south-west of Barcelona. Apart from producing 90 per cent of Spanish sparkling wine (see below), it makes large amounts of still wine, the best of which rivals that from the Rioja. The principal grapes are, for the red wines, the Cariñena, Monastrell, Garnacha tinta and Ull de Llebre (known in the Rioja as the Tempranillo), and for the whites, the Parellada, Xarel-lo and Macabeo (Viura). Apart from these native grapes, Bodegas Torres has successfully acclimatised a number of foreign varieties, including the black Cabernet Sauvignon and Pinot Noir, and the white Chardonnay, Sauvignon blanc, Riesling and Gewürztraminer. The region is best-known for its dry and refreshing white wines, but the reds from Torres, less oaky than most Riojas, are outstanding.

Alella, the most northerly of the demarcated regions in Catalonia is small, with an average production of only 33,000 hectolitres, made in just three bodegas. All the white Alella wines are pleasingly fresh and fruity and bear a passing resemblance to certain Moselles. The approved grape varieties are: for the white wines, Xarel-lo (or Pansa blanca), Pansa rosada and Garnacha blanca; and for the reds, Tempranillo (Ull de Llebre), Garnacha tinta and Garnacha paluda. Julian Jeffs has likened the wines to those from the Loire valley, but adds that 'to compare them with anything is to insult them'. Red Alella is also soft and 'fleshy'; and none of the wines averages more than 12° of alcohol – low for Spain.

As a contrast, Priorato to the south of Barcelona, makes big, strong wines from the Garnacha Negra and Cariñena grapes, almost black in colour, but certainly not lacking in individuality. Their high alcohol content, sometimes approaching 18°, makes them particularly suitable for blending with everyday, non-vintage wines. Although it has become something of a rarity, the region produces a sherry-type wine, matured in pear-shaped glass vessels known as *bombonas* with access to the atmosphere – and for good measure left in the open air.

A further small demarcated region, that of Ampurdán-Costa Brava, abutting the Pyrenees, is best-known for its rosé and sparkling wines, but also makes some very drinkable red wine, fruity and full in body.

Navarra

The southern part of the province, centring on the Ebro Valley and the town of Tudela, produces robust red wines high in alcohol and rather similar in style to those of the Rioja Baja. The best table wines are from the Vinícola Navarra, just south of Pamplona, and from the model estate of the nearby Señorio de Sarría in the valley of the River Arga. Its wines are made from the same grapes as those commonly used in the Rioja: for the reds, a mixture of Tempranillo, Mazuelo, Graciano and Garnacho, with the admixture of a little of the white Malvasia or Viura; for the whites, Viura and Garnacha blanca. All are grown in the Señorio's own vineyards and are matured in oak. The wines, red, white and rosé, are crisp and very drinkable and include first-rate red *reservas*. They may best be compared with the Riojas in style.

Old Castile – León

Although the Ribera del Duero is the most recent region to be demarcated in this large area of northern Spain, it has for long made one of the country's most famous wines.

Vega Sicilia is considered by many connoisseurs to be the best red wine produced in Spain, and the prices certainly match its reputation. Restaurants in London have paid as much for it as for Lafite, and in Spain the problem is to find a restaurant that keeps it, since the output is small and supplies are strictly rationed. It is dark in colour, complex and intensely fruity, with a cedar wood nose, compound of oak and fruit, and long finish. It is also heady to a degree: and the fact that it contains upwards of 13.5° of alcohol would seem to be the exception to the rule of thumb that fine table wines cannot accommodate so high a strength. There is a story that Sir Winston Churchill was served a bottle at the Spanish Embassy in London and singled it out from a choice list by saying that 'My vote goes to this unknown French wine'. It has in fact always been made with grapes from vines of French origin, brought from Bordeaux when the vineyard was devastated by *phylloxera*, in admixture with native varieties. Until recently the French vines were replaced by grafting shoots taken from the vineyards on to American stocks grown in the bodega's nurseries, but quite lately a number of the vineyards have been replanted with Cabernet Sauvignon, Merlot and Malbec obtained directly from nurseries in Montpellier.

Just east of Vega Sicilia, Penafiel produces fruity red wines from the Tinto fino grape, entirely different in character, but much admired by MWs and others since they were first shipped to the UK a few years ago.

The best of the other wines from this part of Spain are from areas to the east and north-east of Valladolid. Rueda, long known for a sherry-like, *flor*-growing wine (see page 17), has recently begun production of young white table wines, dry, fresh and fruity, made mainly from the Verdejo grape. Best-known of these is the white Marqués de Riscal.

León, too, is having considerable success in exporting its wines. The *claretes* from El Bierzo, north of the city of León, have long been favourites with connoisseurs, but are made in very limited amount; and the crisp young red and white 'Rey León' are the first fruits of a very large consortium of growers which has constructed a modern plant to make these and a range of more mature wines aged in oak.

Wine in Bulk

The Spaniards make a broad distinction between *vino corriente* (*vin ordinaire*), drunk regularly and often bought from the barrel, and *vino embotellado*, better quality wine bottled at origin. The distinction has become somewhat blurred with the spread of the supermarket, and most co-operatives now bottle quite ordinary wine. The Ministry of Agriculture classifies wines in somewhat similar terms either as *vinos finos de mesa* (fine table wines) or *vinos comunes*, generally made at a co-operative and sometimes, but by no means always, sold without prior ageing in wood. The fact that a wine has spent a period in cask is of course no guarantee as to its final quality; and conversely, some wines, such as Valdepeñas, are traditionally drunk young, straight from the earthenware *tinaja* or cement tank in which they were made and are none the worse for it. Again, there are smaller bodegas within the area given over to bulk production which produce most individual wines – it would be absurd to classify the excellent peasant-made wine from Salvatierra de Barros in the Extremadura as 'wine in bulk'.

The largest wine-producing area of the country is the central plateau comprising the denominations of Almansa, Manchuela, Mancha, Méntrida and Valdepeñas, between them making some twenty million hectolitres of wine annually. Some 90 per cent of the wine from the central area is white, made from the Airén (or Lairén) grape, drunk under its own name or shipped the length and breadth of Spain for blending. The best of the red wine is from Valdepeñas in the extreme south of La Mancha bordering Andalusia, and made from the black Cencibel (known in the Rioja as the Tempranillo and in Catalonia as the Ull de Llebre). The red wines are full-bodied and go up to 16° in strength, and the whites, pale in colour, average 13° to 14°. Red and white grapes are often mixed to produce wines known as *aloques*, deservedly popular in the bars of Madrid, with their surprising lightness and freshness on the palate.

In the mountains east of La Mancha, the district of Utiel-Requena makes some of the best, lightest and fruitiest rosés in Spain from the black Bobal grape, surprisingly enough produced as a by-product of the thick and highly alcoholic *vino de doble pasta* shipped to other parts of Spain for blending. The central and coastal part of the Province of Valencia is hotter and drier and produces robust wines, red and white, more remarkable for their strength than their delicacy. This tendency is even more marked in Alicante to the south and over the border into Murcia, where Yecla and Jumilla make *vinos valientes* (valiant indeed!) from the black Monastrell grape. The traditional inky black Yecla is for hardened troopers and contains up to 18° of alcohol. That the wines attain so high a strength is because continuous and unbroken sunshine produces abnormally large amounts of sugar in the grapes. Fermentation and break-down of the sugar into alcohol proceeds until the strength approaches a maximum of 18 per cent by volume, beyond which any further concentration paralyses the yeasts. In recent years the huge co-operatives of La Purisima in Yecla and San Isidro in Jumilla, which dominate production in the regions, have been making lighter and less alcoholic wines for export by careful selection of grapes less rich in sugar and by lightening the red wines with a proportion of white.

North of Valencia, the province of Castellón de la Plana

makes a certain amount of robust red wine, pleasant enough for holiday drinking or at a picnic with a slice of cold *tortilla*, but it suffered from being replanted with American hybrids after the disastrous *phylloxera* epidemic. These are now frowned on by the authorities; and because of the expense of replanting with grafted varieties many of its vineyards, including those of the once famous Benicarló, have been abandoned.

Further north along the coast, at the southern extreme of Catalonia, Tarragona is best-known for its dessert wines (see below), but is also the headquarters of numerous huge bodegas blending wines for bulk export. Some of this wine is grown locally and the rest brought in tankers from La Mancha, Utiel, Valencia etc.; most of it is of the type sold abroad in large branded bottles.

Cariñena, near Saragossa in Aragon, has a long and honoured history of wine production and makes a variety of wines, *tintos* and *claretes*, rosés, and white wines ranging from dry and sweet to golden maderised *rancios* rich in alcohol. They are available from supermarkets all over Spain for everyday drinking.

Over to the west, Toro in Old Castile makes somewhat similar *tintos*, deep red in colour, rich in tannin and extract, strong in alcohol, but without much acid; and in the Extremadura, further south and lying along the Portuguese border, the main production centre, resembling nothing so much as an Extremenian Valdepeñas, is Almendralejo, which produces a great deal of sound, but not distinguished, wine for everyday drinking, both red and white, much of it from the white Cayetana grape. Other, more individual wines from the Extremadura are described in the chapter on the different regions.

As a broad generalisation, all the regional bulk-produced wines possess a distinct and well-marked character in their own right.

Green Wines

The west Basque provinces of the north coast make a very limited amount of a thin, slightly *pétillant* wine of only 8° to 9° strength, known as Chacolí. It is not unpleasant at its somewhat steely best, but the best Spanish 'green wines' come from Galicia, which, despite its wet and variable climate is a large producer.

These *vinos verdes* can be compared only with the *vinhos verdes* of the neighbouring region in Portugal (see page 88) which they not unnaturally resemble, since the vines are in some cases the same and the specialised methods of viticulture and viniculture, devised to take maximum advantage of the short summer and limited amount of sun and to eliminate excess acid from the wine, are more or less identical – and, it may be added, in direct contrast to those prevailing in the Rhine valley, where the growers face similar problems.

Low in alcohol, dry to a degree, and sometimes too astringent for those who have not acquired the taste, the white wines are nevertheless delicate, with a flowery bouquet at times resembling that of a Moselle. Indeed, historians have asserted with some confidence that the vines were in the first place brought to Galicia by the Cluniac monks of Santiago de Compostela from the Rhine and Moselle. The best of the wines are the pale yellow Albariños from Fefiñanes, north of Pontevedra, made from the grape of the same name (just as the best *vinhos verdes* are the Alvarinhos from Monção). Although the whites, drunk chilled and with their elusive sparkle, make excellent summer drinking, all but the adventurous student of wine might be advised to leave the reds, tart as they can be, to *aficionados* and the Galicians (who nevertheless drink them with enthusiasm as far afield as Madrid or London).

Dessert Wines

At the opposite end of the pole from the *vinos verdes* are the dessert wines of Málaga, once described by André Simon as 'the perfect "Ladies' Wine" in Victorian days'. In view of the current somewhat illogical fashion for dry wines – it is, in fact, the oldest trick of the trade to serve up a sweetish wine and label it 'dry' – production is now on a reduced scale. Málaga is nowadays made mainly from two types of grape, Pedro Ximénez and Moscatel, grown on the heights to the north and east of the city – hence the old name 'Mountain Wine'. The most luscious of the wines, known as *lágrimas* (or 'tears') are made with the juice emerging from the grapes without mechanical means and as a result of the pressure from the grapes at the top of the load. Málaga wines are aged in *solera* like sherry and Montilla and vary in strength from 15° to 23°. In sweetness they range from dry, pale golden, nutty *amontillados* made from the Pedro Ximénez, to dark, treacly-coloured wines made from sunned Moscatel grapes and sweetened still further by the addition of *arrope* (syrup) made by boiling down must.

Very similar to the rich old Málagas are the *solera*-made Tarragona *clásicos* of firms such as de Muller. These, too, are made from Moscatel or, in the case of the firm's splendid old Priorato *rancios*, from Pedro Ximénez. With long age in *solera* and bottle, the sugar is gradually consumed, so that the flavour becomes bitter-sweet and the finish almost dry.

Another good dessert wine is made around the coastal resort of Sitges, south of Barcelona, from the Moscatel and Malvasía grapes, which are allowed to remain until they wrinkle on the vine, to enhance the sugar content.

Sparkling Wines

Spanish sparkling wines are of three types: an inferior *gasificado*, made in large quantities in Tarragona by pumping carbon dioxide gas into still white wine; a wine made by the *cuve-close* system, in which fermentation takes place in large sealed tanks, producing acceptable results, and of which Perelada from the foothills of the Pyrenees is the best example; and *espumosos* or *cavas* made meticulously by the Champagne method. This last is the system used at San Sadurní de Noya in the Penedès area of Catalonia by numerous firms like Codorníu – whose *cavas* for the production of sparkling wine are reputedly the largest in the world. The wines, though made by the identical process, but not from the same grapes as in Champagne, cannot, as the result of legal action in the UK, be labelled 'Spanish champagne'. In this respect the producers have been less fortunate than the makers of foreign 'sherries', since the best of the Spanish sparkling wines made by the Champagne method from the white Xarel-lo, Macabeo (Viura) and Parellada grapes are first-rate: clean and dry, softer than Champagne, but lacking the edge of the wine produced from the Chardonnay and Pinot Noir grapes grown in the chalky soil of the Marne valley. The South Americans, to whom much of this sparkling wine is exported, have a sweet tooth; so, if you like it dry, it is advisable to ask for the *bruto* or *natur*.

4

Control and Labelling

When Richard Ford rode the length and breadth of Spain between November 1830 and September 1833 to gather the material for his famous *Handbook*, he commented on the very variable quality of Spanish wines: 'The Spaniard himself is neither curious in port, nor particular in Madeira; he prefers quantity to quality, and loves flavour much less than he hates trouble.' Watering and adulteration of wine were rife, so that again he could write: 'The importer will receive the most satisfactory certificates signed and sealed on paper, first duly stamped, in which the alcalde, the muleteer, the guardia, and all who have shared in the booty, will minutely describe and prove the *accident*, be it an upset, a breaking of casks, or what not.'

The Government has long since instituted and enforced regulations for quality control, which find their latest expression in the Ministry of Agriculture's *Estatuto de la Viña, del Vino y de los Alcoholes*. The *Estatuto*, of which some of the main provisions, covering things like the definition of different types of wine, methods of viticulture and vinification, the acceptable tolerance of chemicals and additives and the sale of alcoholic beverages, are summarised in Appendix 4, applies to the country as a whole. To give teeth to its requirements it entrusts their enforcement to *Consejos Reguladores* set up for each of the main wine-growing areas, also listed in Appendix 4. Each of these *Consejos* publishes a detailed *Reglementación* defining the area in which a wine must be produced; the types of grapes, methods of cultivation, vinification and maturing employed in its elaboration; and also limits for the content of alcohol, sugar and acid etc., which must be met if the wine is to qualify for the *Denominación de Origen*. It is this *Denominación de Origen* (corresponding to the French *Appellation d'Origine*), printed on the label with the Consejo's official stamp, that is the consumer's best guarantee as to the authenticity of wine made in the demarcated regions, covering the principal wine-growing areas.

The Consejo Regulador for Rioja, with headquarters at Logrono, is typical of those up and down the country. Its President is nominated by the Ministry of Agriculture; one of its Vice-Presidents is *ex-officio* the Director of the Estación de Viticultura y Enología at Haro and the other a nominee of the

Ministry of Commerce. The other ten members represent the different branches of the local wine community, including the co-operatives.

The old Rioja mark

Attached to the administrative staff are inspectors who carry out regular checks in the vineyards and at the bodegas; and samples of all wine destined for export (but not for domestic consumption) must be lodged with the laboratory at Haro, where they are analysed for density, percentage of alcohol, acid and sugar content etc., and also for the unpermissible 'malvina', an alkaloid colouring matter originating from hybrid American vines. Under its present Director, Don Manuel Ruiz Hernandez, the laboratory has also carried out basic research into the growing, making and maturing of Rioja wines.

If a wine is labelled with a *Denominación de Origen*, the buyer can be confident that it meets the basic standards laid down for its type and region. The guarantee may be printed in the form '*Denominación de Origen Valdepeñas*' or, in the Rioja, the label may carry a small facsimile stamp. Other terms commonly appearing on labels are listed below:

Tinto. Full-bodied red
Clarete. Light red

Rosado. Rosé

Blanco. White

Rancio. Maderised white

Reserva. Mature wine of good quality. *Reserva 1955* refers to wine of that vintage matured in cask and bottle.

Generoso. A fragrant apéritif wine

Espumoso. Sparkling

Vino de mesa, Vino de pasto. Inexpensive table wine

Sangria. Red wine containing citrus juice (see page 58)

Abocado/Dulce. Sweet

Seco. Dry

Brut. Extra-dry (used only of sparkling wines)

4° Año. Bottled during the fourth year after the harvest

Cosecha/Vendimia. Vintage, e.g. *Cosecha 1955*

Viña/Viñedo. Vineyard. Used rather loosely. *Viña Pomal* does not mean that the wine originated exclusively from a vineyard of that name.

Cepa. A vine. Although sometimes coupled with the name of a vine variety, its use on labels is not precise.

Embotellado por . . . Bottled by

Criado por . . . /Elaborado por . . . Matured and/or blended by . . .

Añejo. Old

Añejado por . . . Aged by . . .

Bodega. A concern which may have made, shipped or sold the wine. It normally means that the bodega has made and shipped the wine.

The labels of some of the more select wines like Riscal or Vega Sicilia still carry references to awards or reproductions of the medals gained at the great international wine exhibitions of the 90s and earlier years of the present century. They have been printed as a traditional decoration; but in somewhat spoilsport fashion the EEC now solemnly forbids reference to such hallowed awards on the labels of wines shipped to Common Market countries, so that traditional labels like those of Riscal and Murrieta, by now almost part of the personality of the wine, must now disappear. Of much greater relevance is the EEC requirement that wines be labelled according to the year of vintage and not with a description such as 3° año (meaning simply that it was bottled during the third year after the harvest).

There is no official listing of wines according to quality. The nearest approach is the *Registro Especial de Exportadores*, a pragmatic affair recording the firms, which because of their size and a uniform standard of production in conformity with a *Denominación de Origen*, are licensed to export their wines. The standing of a wine may best be judged by the prices asked over the counter or in a restaurant, or in the case of a less fashionable peasant growth like Cañamero or Montánchez by word of mouth recommendation from the cognoscenti.

Until recently most of the *vino corriente* for everyday drinking was bought from the local bodega – the word means a wine shop as well as a winery. The casks are lined against the wall and chalked on them is a description of their contents, of local origin in wine-growing districts, in such terse terms as *clarete, tinto, blanco* or *rancio* (madeirised white wine), together with the price in pesetas per litre. Customers are expected to bring their own bottles or *botas* (leather wine bags) for replenishment. The present tendency is for wine (of much the same quality) to be bottled at a co-operative and sold in supermarkets. Since wine of this sort is meant for early consumption the bottles are usually not corked, but closed with snap-in plastic inserts before capsuling.

The better quality *vinos embotellados* (bottled wines) are of course obtainable in restaurants and also in bars – where they may be drunk on the spot or taken away – but the best place to buy wine for consumption at home is a good class *ultramarino* (or grocer). Bottled table wine is no longer the bargain that it used to be in Spain; but the fine Riojas are still good value in comparison with wine of similar quality from France or Germany. As in other countries, prices are much marked up in expensive hotels.

It is perhaps of interest to the visitor that the *Estatuto de la Viña* empowers the Government to fix maximum retail prices for bottled wines appropriate to the category of the establishment, and all restaurants serving either *table d'hôte* or *à la carte* meals are obliged to produce this list on demand. Prices in the government-run Paradors and Albergues have always been reasonable; and unlike many other hotels of similar standing they offer generous *jarras* (carafes) or inexpensive local wine, both red and white. In wine-growing areas like the Rioja the quality is excellent.

5

The Regions

Spain is much too large a country to plan a tour of all its wine-growing areas during a single holiday. To attempt it would simply be to spend most of the time on the road without gaining any real insight into the different regions, so variegated in their scenery, history and culture. The most fervent wine-lover would be blind indeed if he did not turn aside to visit the prehistoric caves at Altamira, the cathedral at Santiago de Compostela, the Monastery of Guadelupe, the Roman Theatre at Mérida or the Great Mosque at Córdoba – to mention only a few of the most noteworthy sights. And even the wine tastes better after an energetic morning at the Alhambra and the gardens of the Generalife!

More specifically, a knowledge of the wines is acquired in various ways: by tastings and visits to bodegas when these can be arranged, by inspection of the vineyards as you drive by and, perhaps most important, by a more leisurely savouring and appraisal over a pleasant meal. The network of government-run Paradors and Albergues offers comfortable rooms and good regional food and wines even in the most remote districts. The Paradors are often installed in carefully restored castles, monasteries and palaces and are generally more luxurious than the Albergues, which are of modern construction, though this is not always so. There are, of course, also wine museums, though none as rewarding as that of Vilafranca de Penedès near Barcelona – few exercises are more frustrating than surveying the inaccessible bottles (their contents, no doubt, long turned to vinegar) of the typical local museum.

If you fly to Spain, or go by boat or train, the first essential is a car, since many of the vineyards and bodegas are off the beaten track, and cross country journeys from one to another present difficulties in a country where all the main lines of communication radiate from Madrid. Local buses are infrequent and slow, though for *aficionados* they have their compensations: the peasant woman with whose coop of chickens you share your seat will probably offer you a slice of cold tortilla and *vino corriente* from a *bota*. It is in fact often cheaper and more convenient to hire a small car on the spot than to make the long drive overland. It is possible to hire a car

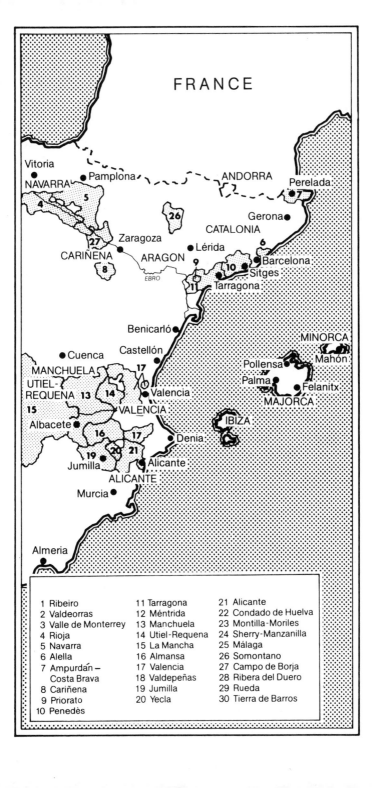

FRANCE

Vitoria
NAVARRA ● Pamplona
ANDORRA
Perelada ●7

4 5
26
Gerona ●
CATALONIA

27
Zaragoza ● Lérida
CARIÑENA ARAGON 9 6
8 EBRO 10 Barcelona
11 Sitges
Tarragona

Benicarló ●

● Cuenca Castellón ●
MINORCA
MANCHUELA 17 Pollensa ● Mahón ●
UTIEL- 14 Palma ● Felanitx ●
REQUENA 13 Valencia MAJORCA
15 VALENCIA
Albacete ●
16
17 Denia ● IBIZA
19 20 21
Jumilla Alicante ●
ALICANTE

Murcia ●

Almeria ●

1 Ribeiro	11 Tarragona	21 Alicante
2 Valdeorras	12 Méntrida	22 Condado de Huelva
3 Valle de Monterrey	13 Manchuela	23 Montilla-Moriles
4 Rioja	14 Utiel-Requena	24 Sherry-Manzanilla
5 Navarra	15 La Mancha	25 Málaga
6 Alella	16 Almansa	26 Somontano
7 Ampurdán – Costa Brava	17 Valencia	27 Campo de Borja
8 Cariñena	18 Valdepeñas	28 Ribera del Duero
9 Priorato	19 Jumilla	29 Rueda
10 Penedès	20 Yecla	30 Tierra de Barros

at one centre and hand it in at another; and some of the airlines offer advantageous all-in schemes.

Some people will of course prefer to drive through France or to put the car on the overnight ferry to Santander. From here to Bilbao the 109 kilometres are tortuous and slow, but Bilbao is only 1½ to 2 hours' drive to Haro or Logroño in the Rioja by way of the new A68 motorway. By striking diagonally across France and entering Spain at the southern end of the Pyrenees you are well placed for exploring Catalonia; and this has the additional advantage of allowing direct comparison between the quality and prices of wine either side of the border.

Visiting Wineries

If you wish to visit any but the larger bodegas where there are regular arrangements for receiving visitors, it is more or less essential to speak some Spanish. The best organised centre is Jerez de la Frontera, where anyone is welcome at the large sherry bodegas during visiting hours without prior appointment and English-speaking guides are provided. Some of the larger bodegas in the Rioja are also prepared for visitors, as are well-known establishments like Chartreuse in Tarragona or the *cavas* at San Sadurní de Noya, where Codorníu make their sparkling wines; but it is always sensible to check beforehand. Ask at the reception desk of your hotel or get the hall porter to telephone. At smaller bodegas in the Rioja and elsewhere it is understandable enough that there is no staff available to look after unannounced callers, though they are pleased enough to receive visitors armed with a letter of introduction from their shippers, which always ensures special treatment.

At small peasant bodegas or country co-operatives, no preliminaries are necessary beyond turning up and speaking the language. The Spaniards are friendly people and if not in the throes of weighing grapes or other essential business will take a pride in doing the honours of the establishment and offering samples of their wine. Bear in mind, however, that such rustic bodegas are largely unoccupied except at harvest time, and it is as well to remember that all concerns in Spain, shops and offices included, are shut during the lunch and siesta hours of 1 p.m. to 4 p.m. (or 1.30 p.m. to 4.30 p.m. or 5 p.m. in summer). As a footnote, some tourist agencies offer group tours of the Rioja with organised tastings and guided tours of the bodegas. Details may be obtained from the Spanish National Tourist Office, 57 St James's Street, London SW1, or from travel agents.

In planning a tour the first thing is to look at a map and to decide how much ground you wish to cover and what other general sightseeing is to be included. The 1:1,000,000 Michelin sheet of Spain and Portugal is useful for general purposes and the 1:1,500,000 *Mapas de Carreteras* published by Firestone Hispania for more detailed exploration of individual regions. The suggested routes for adjacent regions may be combined; or again you may prefer to settle by the sea and to limit your excursions to places within easy reach.

For descriptive purposes the country can be divided into six main regions: Andalusia; Levante and New Castile; Catalonia; Aragón and Navarra; the Rioja and Old Castile; Galicia; and Extremadura. These embrace thirty-two demarcated wine-growing areas, listed in Appendix 4. The Balearics are not of outstanding interest for their wines, but are best reached either from Barcelona or by a direct flight from abroad.

Andalusia

Although there are direct flights to Málaga in the east, the best centre is Seville, accessible from Madrid by air, by the main N.4 road to the south or by the fast and comfortable Talgo train. Do not leave without seeing the cathedral and its one-time minaret, the Giralda; the Alcázar palace and its Moorish gardens; or eating in the open air at one of the restaurants of the Calle de Sierpes, with its overhead awning.

If you wish to make a complete tour of the wine-growing areas, take the N.4 or new motorway through the sherry vineyards to Jerez de la Frontera. Stay in Jerez, visit the bodegas, and make side trips to the wine towns of Sanlúcar de Barrameda, 23 km to the north, and Puerto de Santa María, about the same distance on the main road south to Cadiz. From Jerez, take the N.4, N.33 and N.334 to Antequera and lunch at the excellent government-run Parador, just recently opened there. Continue by the N.331 and N.321 and stay in Málaga for visits to the bodegas in the city and the surrounding vineyards. Return to Antequera. Either stay here and visit Montilla, off the N.331 to Córdoba, or make your base for Montilla-Moriles in Córdoba itself, preferably at the spacious Parador of Arruzafa, above the city and adjacent to the impressive ruins of the Moorish palace of Madinat al-Zahra. The cathedral, formerly the Great Mosque, and the old Jewish quarter are a must. From Córdoba you can return to Madrid direct by train or the N.4, or break your journey in Valdepeñas, the wine centre of La Mancha.

To see the vineyards of Huelva, you must make a long side trip in the other direction from Seville, to the west; in this case the pleasantest places to stay are the seaside Paradors of either Ayamonte or Mazagón, both near Huelva. Once in this direction, it is worth branching off on the C.445, 55 km along the N.431 from Seville, for a visit to the remarkable nature reserve of the Coto Donana on the Guadalquivir estuary.

THE SHERRY REGION

Jerez de la Frontera is no longer quite the idyllic place that it was. Like other sizable Spanish towns, it is now ringed with high-rise apartments and factories and its one-way streets are jammed with traffic. However, the narrow alleys and white-washed houses of the old town, with their balconies riotous with geraniums, still survive, as do the great bodegas with their countless thousands of butts of maturing wine – the lifeblood of the town. One of the saddest casualties has been the Los Cisnes Hotel, old-fashioned but elegant and full of atmosphere with its patio and great yellow awning, where one ate in summer. Its place has been taken by the modern Hotel Jerez further out, air-conditioned with a large garden and swimming pool, and following in the traditions of Los Cisnes in that its lounge bar is a crossroads of Jerez society before dinner. An agreeable alternative is the Parador of the Casa del Corregidor, perched high above the gorge of the Guadalete some 30 km to the east in the old Moorish town of Arcos de la Frontera.

The liveliest time for a visit is during the Fiesta of the Vendimia, held at the weekend nearest 8 September, the official date for the beginning of the harvest, and dedicated to a country or city where sherry is popular. Celebrations start on the Friday with a grand procession in honour of the Queen of the Vintage, who drives through the streets on a float decorated with grapes, accompanied by her maids of honour, chosen from the dark beauties of Andalusia, arrayed in white dresses and blue silk scarves. Festivities continue during the next few days with ceremonies at the Bodega of San Ginés – in effect a museum of viticulture – bullfights, horse shows, flamenco dancing and fireworks, culminating on the Sunday with the blessing of the grapes and the release of doves when the first juice runs out of the old-fashioned presses arranged on the steps of the Collegiate Church. Accommodation is of course at a premium and the bodegas are closed to visitors at fiesta time, so that if you have come for more leisurely and serious study of the wines, it is better to choose another period.

Entering the great nave of one of the sherry cathedrals, as Richard Ford called the bodegas, the visitor's first impression is of mountainous butts of wine peacefully awaiting their time in an atmosphere of religious gloom. The elaboration of sherry is nevertheless a highly complex business; the guides, who are uniformed in the grander establishments and deliver their commentary in various languages for the benefit of different members of the party, are helpful and informative, but it is useful to have a grasp of the subject beforehand.

The vineyards are parcelled out into areas known as *pagos* belonging to the different proprietors and the best are those of

Macharnudo and Carrascal, to the north; Añina, Balbaina and Los Tercios, to the west; and further afield near Sanlúcar de Barrameda, those of Miraflores, producing the grapes for the *manzanillas*. There are other isolated areas to the east; but the wines from Chiclana, beyond Cadiz to the south are not of the same quality and used for blending. The best of the soils, though least prolific in terms of yield, is the dazzling, chalky *albariza*. Dotted among the vineyards you may occasionally still see the *bienteveos*, rough shelters made of poles roofed with esparto grass matting. The word means 'I see you well', and there is a proverb in Jerez:

> *Las niñas y las viñas difíciles son de guardar*
> (Girls and vineyards are difficult to guard)

The *bienteveos* in fact date from a time when they were manned by armed guards, who would shoot on sight thieves helping themselves to the ripe grapes.

The grapes are nowadays picked into plastic containers holding 17 kg and small enough to avoid bruising or rupture of the grapes and premature fermentation of the must. They were formerly laid out on esparto grass mats and sunned, so as to concentrate the juice by evaporation. Thanks to more precise laboratory methods for judging the optimum point for picking, sunning is now not much used except for grapes intended for sweet wines; and the laden boxes of fruit arrive at the bodega by lorry, often within half-an-hour of being picked.

During a visit to the bodegas you will almost certainly be shown the *zapatos de pisar*, cowhide boots studded with flat-headed tacks, which were formerly worn by the labourers to crush the grapes in wooden troughs before the must was run off into the wine press. It was a picturesque ceremony and an effective means of avoiding the splitting open of stalks and pips, which would otherwise have resulted in an undue proportion of tannin in the wine. It has now been abandoned in favour of horizontal presses first devised in Germany, which achieve the same result at vastly less expense. They work by squeezing the grapes against the sides of a stainless steel cylinder by means of a strong rubber bag, so avoiding crushing of the pips and stems and the process is repeated until all the juice has been released. In an even more modern type of continuous crusher, the fruit is fed into a long inclined Archimedean screw; the must which first separates is used for *finos*, and that obtained later with more pressure, for *olorosos*.

Some of the bodegas, like Sandemans, ferment the fresh must traditional style in oak butts; others use stainless steel tanks, with the advantage of stricter control of temperature; while others again, like Garveys and CAYD, ferment in the cement *tinajas* familiar in Montilla. Whatever the method, secondary fermentation is over by December or January, when the must 'falls bright' and is ready to begin the years' long processes of maturing, blending and fortification.

The most important fact to grasp about sherry is that, unlike most wines, it is fermented and matures in loosely stoppered butts with free access to the atmosphere. The normal result of exposing wine to air for any considerable time is to turn it to vinegar through the agency of a bacterium known as *Mycoderma aceti* – and this is in fact how vinegar is made commercially. In Jerez de la Frontera the young wines possess the astonishing property of growing a *flor* on the liquid interface. Although the word means a 'flower', the *flor* is in fact an unsightly, wrinkled layer of yeasts of the genus *Saccharomyces*, which both regulates the access of air to the developing must and at the same time prevents the growth of the vinegar-producing bacterium. As the wine grows older and stronger in alcohol, the *flor* becomes thinner and eventually sinks to the bottom of the butt; and some sherries, particularly the *olorosos*, produce little or none of it at all.

Richard Ford's description of the *solera* system by which the wine is produced still remains the neatest:

> The contents of one barrel serve to correct another until the proposed standard aggregate is produced; and to such certainty has this uniform admixture been reduced, that houses are enabled to supply for any number of years exactly that particular colour, flavour, body etc., which particular customers demand. The wine improves very much with age, gets softer and more aromatic and gains both body and aroma, in which its younger wines are deficient.

Once the wine has been racked free of solid matter, sparingly fortified and classified according to one of the types already described (page 15), it is described as *sobre tabla* and is ready to begin its education in the *solera*. The word comes from the Latin *solum* or Spanish *suelo* and applies strictly to the row of butts at floor level containing the oldest wine, but more loosely to the whole assemblage of casks from which this *solera* proper is replenished. The rows of casks from which the *solera* is fed are collectively known as the *criadera* and consist of 'scales' containing wine of the same type, but progressively younger in age. The procedure is to draw off wine from the butts first laid down, which are then 'refreshed' with rather less mature wine, and so on down all the 'scales' to the youngest wine in the *criadera*. This process is practical because the younger wine rapidly takes on the character of the older.

A typical *solera* with its *criadera* might contain some five 'scales'; to make *manzanilla* as many as fourteen are employed, and the operation is somewhat different. The *solera* system is also employed in Jerez de la Frontera for making Spanish brandy.

Before bottling, the wine was traditionally cleared with egg white and 'Spanish earth'; but the large bodegas now use refrigeration plant for clarifying it and precipitating the crystals of potassium bitartrate, which might otherwise separate out in cold climates. As already noted, most sherries are not straight *solera* wines, but blends. At some of the bodegas they will allow you to sip the black, bitter wine, first laid down a century or so ago and undrinkable on its own, which is used in minimal amounts to confer edge and flavour. When one of the lighter sherries is intended for export, the final stage of blending is a further slight fortification with *mitad y mitad*, a fifty-fifty mixture of alcohol and sherry. This is done to prevent the possible development of cloudiness or deposit and, in the case of a *fino*, to avoid risk of the reappearance of the *flor*.

The operation of the *solera* is entrusted to the *capataz* or cellar-man, whose chosen instrument for sampling the wine is the *venencia*. In Jerez, this picturesque and elegant instrument consists of a long flexible whalebone handle with a silver cup at one end and a decorative hook, also of solid silver, at the other. In Sanlúcar it is made from a piece of bamboo, a hollow section

Sherry taster using a venencia

of which serves as the cup, while the yard-long handle is pared away to a thickness of about quarter-of-an-inch. Both are plunged into the butt through the bung-hole and are designed to avoid undue disturbance of the *flor*. The dexterity of the *capataz* is astonishing, and to entertain visitors he will sometimes hold a bevy of glasses in the same hand, while at the same time directing jets of wine into them with unerring accuracy. It is of interest that his judgment of the wine is usually based on the appraisal of bouquet alone and not on tasting, as with most other wines.

Towards the end of the visit you will be shown butts of wine laid down in honour of visiting royalty, statesmen and other celebrities, with their names prominent on the ends of the casks; and the final port of call is always the *salón de degustación*, a comfortably laid out bar with chairs and tables, where the wine may be savoured at leisure in the appropriate tulip-shaped glasses. The sherry concerns are generous to their visitors; and this is the opportunity to taste all the wines from the pale and delicate *finos* to the full-bodied dessert *olorosos* – trying them, of course, in that order. The overriding impression is of the boundless freshness and fragrance of wine that has not travelled or been subjected to the vagaries of standing on a wine shop's shelves for uncertain periods.

At the sherry bodegas the *fino* wines are served from chilled half bottles to ensure that they are fresh; unfortunately this is not the general practice in bars and hotels up and down the country, where the *fino* is too often served at room temperature – sometimes high – from a half empty bottle. This is not of so much account with an *oloroso*, which in its sweetened form is little drunk in Spain and almost never by the Spanish male, who, if he is taking sherry, will generally ask for a *fino* before a meal and drink brandy afterwards. The best-known brands of dessert sherry are nevertheless obtainable in many bars and sweet *oloroso* is also available from the barrel (*a granel*) in old-fashioned bodegas (in the sense of the traditional wine shop). Here you should ask for it as 'Jerez dulce'.

If bars in general are not over careful in the way they keep their sherry, it is at least served in the traditional long in-curving *copita* (a diminutive of *copa*, a glass). This should be only half-filled, so that the full aroma of the wine may be appreciated (when sherry is served in a glass like this it is easy to understand why the *capataz* has need of no more than his nose). Other wines are, incidentally, often served in small and solid tumblers – a pity in the case of a good table wine, which responds to the warmth of the hand and of which the bouquet can best be appreciated in the larger, tall inwardly curving glass, half-filled, such as those used in the Rioja and at better restaurants. Wines from the barrel are served in *jarras* (or jugs) rather than in carafes. Usually of brown glazed earthenware, with the name of the establishment in white, they are made in various sizes in the potteries of places like Talavera de la Reina and Manises and are often very decorative.

As to the practical details of a visit, no advance notice is necessary at the larger and better-known sherry bodegas. Visiting hours are usually between 10 a.m. and 1.30 p.m., when the staff goes to lunch. Since the tour and tasting take about an hour, turn up by noon at the latest. During the holiday season you will be asked to wait and to join a party; at other times the trip may well be individual. As regards tipping the guides you must use your own judgment; all are provided by the bodegas, but whereas a uniformed guide will gladly accept a tip and indeed expect it, a member of the bodega's office staff might well be put out.

Many of the bodegas possess decorative gardens and patios and all have special points of interest. For example, at Gonzalez Byass a quaint feature are the tiny sherry-fed mice; at Harvey's there is a pool in the garden inhabited by an alligator; Zoilo Ruiz-Mateus houses a splendid collection of antique clocks; others, like Bodegas Internacionales, stand out for sheer size and modernity; while at Williams and Humbert you will see the former office of the British consul, traditionally located there. Until recently British-owned, this was one of the sixteen bodegas in Jerez to be taken over by RUMASA. Starting in Jerez with the firm of Zoilo Ruiz-Mateus, it embraced banks, insurance, shipping, chemicals, hotels and property, as well as other large sectors of the wine industry, but has recently and dramatically been expropriated.

There are some fifty bodegas in Jerez de la Frontera; among those prepared for visits, and whose addresses may be checked from the telephone directory or at the reception desk of your hotel, are:

Pedro Domecq, S.A.
Garvey, S.A. Co. Ltd.
Gonzales Byass y Cía., S.L.
Sandeman Hermanos y Cía., S.R.C.
Williams & Humbert Ltd.

In Puerto de Santa María, from which much of the wine was formerly shipped, bodegas which may be visited without special appointment are:

Fernando A. de Terry, S.R.C.
Osborne y Cía., S.A.

Some other well-known houses in Jerez and Puerto de Sta. María, whose wines are shipped to Britain, are:

Bertola, S.A.
Agustín Blázquez
Bobadilla y Cía., Ltda.
Bodegas Internacionales, S.A.

Croft, Jerez, S.A.
Cuvillo y Cía
Duff Gordon y Cía, S.A.
John Harvey & Sons Ltd.
Emilio Lustau, S.A.
Marqués del Real Tesoro, S.A.
Palomino y Vergara, S.A.
M. Antonio de la Riva, S.A.
Zoilo Ruiz-Mateos, S.A.
A. R. Valdespino, S.A.

It is a particularly pleasant excursion to drive through the vineyards to Sanlúcar de Barrameda, to taste the *manzanilla* in its native surroundings and to lunch at one of the shellfish bars overlooking the wide Guadalquivir estuary. You will need an introduction to visit the bodegas, numbering some dozen, of which the best-known are:

A. Barbadillo, S.A.
C.A.Y.D., S.A.
Hijos de Pérez Marín, S.A.

MONTILLA-MORILES

Although the region produces only about half as much wine, very similar in style to sherry, the demarcated area is almost as large as that of Jerez, and is one of the sunniest and hottest in Spain. The most southerly production centres, like Lucena and Puente Genil, are nearer Antequera than Córdoba; but probably the best place to study the making of the wine is Montilla itself, just off the N.331 some 44 km south of Córdoba. Moriles is only a tiny village on a side road west of Lucena; and Montilla, the Munda Betica of the Romans and the scene of fierce fighting when Julius Caesar destroyed the remains of Pompey's armies, although a town of some 30,000 people and one of the most attractive in Andalusia, possesses no hotel. The main road from Antequera to Córdoba, suggested in the itinerary, will take you through the heart of the hilly wine-growing area, with the predominant Pedro Ximénez vines grown low in the chalky white *Albero* soil.

Apart from being smaller, the bodegas differ from those of Jerez in that fermentation is traditionally carried out in large bulbous earthenware *tinajas*, resembling in shape the Roman *orcae* or *amphorae* from which they are descended, fabricated on the spot and arranged in long rows with access from a raised wooden platform. In the larger, more modern bodegas these are now being replaced by cement vats. During the first stage of tumultuous fermentation the tops are left open, but as the temperature drops and the gas stops coming off, they are covered wth wooden lids. The turbid liquid then begins to clear and within a few months is completely clear and transparent, when it is either drawn off into oak butts and either sold as *vino corriente* or removed to one of the large *bodegas de crianza* in Montilla or Córdoba.

The finer wines are matured in *soleras* like those of Jerez – except that, as already mentioned, they are never brandied. Like sherry, they grow a *flor*, and after the attentions of the *capataz* emerge as one of the types specified by the Consejo Regulador and listed in the table. The typical type is the dry *fino*, always drunk chilled.

Type of wine	% Alcohol by volume	Characteristics
Fino	14–17.5	Pale and dry with a greenish tint, slightly bitter, light and fragrant on the palate.
Amontillado	16–18, rising to 20 when very old	Amber-coloured, dry 'nutty' flavour, combining age and finesse.
Oloroso	16–18, rising to 20 when very old	Mahogany-coloured, full-bodied and velvety, highly aromatic, dry or with a hint of sweetness.
Palo Cortado	16–18	Midway between the *amontillado* and *oloroso*, with the pungent bouquet of the former and the unmistakable flavour of *oloroso*.
Raya	16–18	Generally similar to *oloroso*, but with less quality and bouquet.
Pedro Ximénez		A sweet, fortified wine, dark ruby in colour.

Some important bodegas are:

Alvear, S.A., Montilla
Aragón y Cía., Lucena
Carbonell y Cía., Córdoba
Gracia Hermanos, S.A.
Monte Cristo, S.A.
Montulia, S.A.
Pérez Barquero, S.A.

HUELVA

This makes up the trio of the regions producing *flor*-growing wines markedly similar to sherry and matured in a *solera*. In fact, of some 800,000 hectolitres annually produced in the demarcated area, only about 130,000 are *vinos generosos* of this type, the great bulk being white wine, much of it destined for distillation. Pedro Domecq, for example, operate one of the distilleries for making the *holandas* or grape spirit for their brandies at Bollullos del Condado. The Condado is that of the Guzmán counts, famous in Spanish history; and Bollullos (at the junction of the N.431 from Seville and the C.445, running down to the salt marshes of the *Marismas* and the nature reserve of the Coto Doñana) also possesses *bodegas de crianza* for maturing sherry-type wines. The others are located in the villages further west towards the town of Huelva. You should taste them on the spot, since the bulk of production goes to Jerez for blending.

MÁLAGA

The vineyards, small in size, are mostly in the hills to the north and east of Málaga: around Antequera on the suggested itinerary; near Archidona on the N.342 from Antequera to Granada; around Vélez-Málaga, up from the N.340, the main coast road from Valencia and the north; and in the Sierra Almijara above Nerja, with its pleasant modern Parador. All are within easy driving distance of Torremolinos and the other holiday resorts of the Costa del Sol. An agreeable resting place in Málaga is the Parador of Gibralfaro, with its splendid view of the old Moorish castle and terraces overlooking the city and bay.

The wine is made either in the small bodegas of the mountain villages or in establishments near the vineyards owned by the large firms, such as Scholtz and Barceló, where it is fermented in large cylindrical cement containers, resembling the *tinajas* of Montilla, but rounded at the bottom. The new wine is then brought into the city by tanker lorry, where it must in any case be matured to qualify for *Denominación de Origen* – although it is a sign of the times that in a region which now lives on tourism, even the famous Scholtz Hermanos have perforce emigrated to the outskirts. Maturation is in *soleras* operated like those in Jerez and Montilla. Again as in Jerez, the grapes are sun-dried for the sweeter wines, which are laced with an *arrope* (or syrup) made by evaporating down unfermented must in a copper pan and adding alcohol to prevent subsequent fermentation.

Perhaps the best way to sample Málagas in their variety is at one of the bars in the centre of the city, where they are served from the wood. By no means all are sticky-sweet, and the best, like the beautiful Scholtz Solera 1885, well merit Harry Yoxall's evocative description in *Wine & Food*: 'There are interesting, almost surprising undertones beneath its unctuous richness, like the dark fires in the heart of a jewel. Just as the touch of something very cold leaves you uncertain whether it has frozen or burnt you, so in the taste of great Málagas the sugar is sublimated and becomes almost astringent.'

The Rioja

The most direct approach to the Rioja is by car ferry to Santander, or by air to Bilbao, where self-drive cars may be hired. From Bilbao take the A.68 motorway, following signs for Logroño, which is about two hours' drive along an impressively engineered route, first climbing high through the mountains and entering the Rioja through the gorge of the Conchas de Haro. It takes longer from Santander than would appear from a map, since the scenic N.634 coast road to Bilbao, much used by heavy lorries, is sinuous and hilly and Bilbao itself is always congested.

The bodegas are thickest on the ground in and around the small town of Haro, but the centre of the Rioja wine trade is the larger Logroño, a natural starting point for a visit to the district. It possesses a number of comfortable hotels, the favourite of the wine trade being the Murrieta; if you wish to stay out of the city, there is the Parador of Santo Domingo de la Calzada, 19 km south of Haro, in mediaeval times a hostel for pilgrims en route for Santiago de Compostela.

A bird's eye view of the most important wine-growing areas may be obtained by making the circuit from Logroño to Haro and back by the roads to the north and south of the Ebro – only some 100 km in all. Cross the bridge over the Ebro and, passing the Bodegas Franco Españolas, branch left on to the N.232 for Laguardia. Turn up the steep hill into the walled mediaeval town, park your car where you can and explore its narrow alleys, churches, old dark houses and peasant bodegas. Resume the N.232 to the wine village of Labastida, passing through the vineyards of Bodegas Santiago, and at Briñas turn sharp left down the steep hill into Haro. This will take you past a number of the best-known bodegas, including Bilbainas, Muga, CVNE and Santiago. Visit one or more of the bodegas in the town – an introduction or prior telephone call is advisable. Lunch at the scrubbed wooden tables of Terete (its address is General Franco, 26), preferably off the baby lamb (*lechazo*) roasted in its baker's oven and choosing from its excellent list of Riojas. If you want to buy some Rioja, the shop of Juan Gonzalez Muga in the main square specialises in old and rare vintages and also offers special purchases from the bodegas at bargain prices.

Head out of Haro by the southern branch of the N.232 for Briones. This walled, hill-top township just off the main road is one of the most picturesque in the region and is worth visiting both for the church and seignorial houses, and for the splendid view over the River Ebro. The road continues up and down hill, at times within sight of the Ebro and passing through the vineyards, and finally takes you back to Logroño via another two important wine-making centres, Cenicero and Fuenmayor.

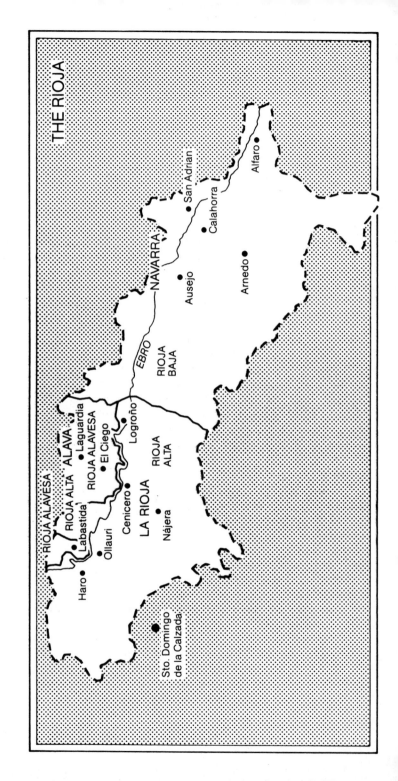

Alternatively, you may turn left at Cenicero and return via Laguardia. The 11 km of this country road are particularly interesting. In Cenicero are the large bodegas of Riojanas and Berberana; and continuing over the bridge across the Ebro, the road passes the new building of Salceda, the vineyards and bodegas of the Marqués de Riscal at Elciego and, just short of Laguardia, the new installations of Bodegas Alavesas and of Bodegas Palacio, now owned by Seagrams.

To explore a wine-growing district as important as the Rioja in any depth you should spend a number of days – though it is hardly worth devoting much time to the Rioja Baja to the east of Logroño, and if you continue into Catalonia via the A.68 motorway or the N.232, if you wish to proceed at a more leisurely pace and see the countryside, you will in any case pass through Calahorra, Alfaro and the vineyards bordering the Ebro.

The liveliest time to visit Logroño – though not the best for visiting the bodegas – is during the week-long Fiesta of San Mateo, beginning on September 21st, rather before grape-picking, which traditionally starts on 10 October. The *bodegueros* (proprietors) and their workers flood into the city to watch the bullfights and the uniformed bands parading the streets, to eat at trestle tables in the small streets sloping down to the river, or foregather in the evening at the open-air cafés of the tree-lined Plaza del Espolón to see the huge clusters of fireworks bursting in the mild, still air. But if you want to take part in the celebrations, it is essential to book your hotel well in advance.

To help plan an itinerary, here is a list of the large *Bodegas de Exportación*:

BODEGAS OF THE RIOJA ALTA

AGE, Bodegas Unidas (Azpilicueta, Cruz García and Entrena)	Fuenmayor and Navarrete
Bodegas Berberana	Cenicero and Ollauri
Bodegas Beronia	Ollauri
Bodegas Bilbainas	Haro
Bodegas Campo Viejo (Savin)	Logroño
Bodegas Carlos Serres, Hijo	Haro
Bodegas Cooperativas Sta. María la Real	Nájera
Bodegas Corral	Navarrete
Bodegas Delicia	Ollauri
Bodegas Francisco Viguera	Haro
Bodegas Franco Españolas (RUMASA)	Logroño
Bodegas Gómez Cruzado	Haro
Bodegas La Rioja Alta	Haro
Bodegas Lafuente	Fuenmayor
Bodegas Lagunilla (IDV)	Cenicero

Bodegas Lan	Fuenmayor
Bodegas López Agos	Fuenmayor
Bodegas Olarra	Logroño
Bodegas Marqués de Caceres	Cenicero
Bodegas Marqués de Murrieta	Ygay
Bodegas Martínez Lacuesta Hnos.	Haro
Bodegas Montecillo (Osborne)	Fuenmayor
Bodegas Muga	Haro
Federico Paternina, Vinos Rioja S.A.	Ollauri
Bodegas R. López de Heredia, Viña Tondonia	Haro
Bodegas Ramón Bilbao	Haro
Bodegas Real Divisa	Abalos
Bodegas Rioja Santiago (Pepsi-Cola)	Haro
Bodegas Riojanas	Cenicero
Bodegas Velázquez	Cenicero
Bodegas Vista Alegre	Haro
Castillo de Cuzcurrita	Rio Tirón
Compañía Vinícola del Norte de España (CVNE)	Haro

BODEGAS OF THE RIOJA ALAVESA

Bodegas Alavesas	Laguardia
Bodegas Cantabria	Laguardia
Bodegas Cooperativa Vinícola de Labastida	Labastida
Bodegas Domeqc, S.A.	
Bodegas Faustino Martínez	Oyón
Bodegas Palacio (Seagram)	Laguardia
Bodegas Rojas y Cía.	Laguardia
Bodegas Viña Salceda	Elciego
Rioja Alavesa SMS	Villabuena
Vinos de los Herederos del Marqués de Riscal	Elciego

BODEGAS OF THE RIOJA BAJA

Bodegas Gurpegui	San Adrián
Bodegas Latorre y Lapuerta	Alfaro
Bodegas Muerza	San Adrián
Bodegas Palacios, Vino Rioja	Alfaro
Bodegas Rivero	Arnedo
Savin, S.A.	Aldeanueva del Ebro

If you have the opportunity, it is interesting to visit at least one of the old-established medium-sized bodegas and, as a contrast, one of the vast modern installations. The main difference is in scale and in the modernity of the equipment used for vinifying the wine in the new establishments, with their serried rows of stainless steel tanks and computerised consoles for controlling operations from the arrival of the grapes to the making of the wine. Thereafter, whatever the size of the bodega, the wine must be matured in traditional fashion in 225-litre *barricas* if it is to be sold as Rioja *con crianza* ('with ageing').

Typical of the traditional medium-sized bodegas are López de Heredia, C.V.N.E. (Compañia Vinícola del Norte de España) and Bodegas La Rioja Alta in Haro or the famous Marqués de Riscal in Elciego and Marqués de Murrieta in Ygay, just outside Logroño. The biggest of the new plants are those of Federico Paternina just outside Haro (formerly owned by RUMASA, which also controlled Franco Españolas in Logroño and Berberana in Cenicero), and the great new bodega of Olarra on the outskirts of Logroño, shaped like a star to symbolise the three sub-regions of the Rioja Alta, Rioja Alavesa and Rioja Baja.

MAKING THE WINE

If you wish to see the vinification of the grapes, plan the visit for mid-October. In the past, vineyards were often planted with different varieties of grape in the proportions used in the wine, so that all the grapes were picked and fermented together. This had the disadvantage that some varieties, like the Tempranillo, ripened before others; and the Consejo Regulador now stipulates that in new plantations different varieties must be grown apart. Where the different grape varieties are separately fermented, the musts are later blended.

They are first crushed to liberate the juice, care being taken to reject the stalks and to avoid splitting the pips, which would result in the release of excessive amounts of tannin and vegetable oils. The must is now pumped to the fermentation vats, the procedure differing according to the type of wine. The fuller-bodied *tinto* is fermented in contact with the skins and most of the pips, while the *clarete* is left in contact with the skins for a shorter period during fermentation, so that less of the colouring matter and tannin – which originate in the skins and pips, and not the juice – pass into the wine. Both are fully fermented as regards conversion of sugar into alcohol, but the *tinto* contains more tannin and acid and emerges as a darker, fuller-bodied and longer-living wine. White wines are femented without the skins and pips, which are removed after the crushing of the grapes, and fermentation is sometimes cut short so as to leave some of the grape sugar in the sweeter wines.

Tumultuous fermentation lasts for about three days and in the older bodegas is carried out in large *cubas* (vats) made of American or Canadian oak, which may be of various shapes and sizes, and are filled four-fifths to allow for the 'seething' caused by the brisk evolution of carbon dioxide, as the sugars are broken down through the agency of the yeasts present in the bloom on the skins of the grapes. In many of the modern bodegas the oak vats have now been replaced by vats or tanks of cement, stainless steel or steel coated with epoxy resin. The advantage of the metal tanks is that they are hygienic and that the temperature of fermentation may be controlled by running cold water over the outside. This is particularly important in making the new-style white wines, which may be fermented for as long as six weeks at temperatures of around 16°C, so as to conserve the fruity nose and flavour.

The next step is to run the new wine out of the vat and in the case of the reds to free them from skins and pips. This is traditionally done in a hydraulic basket press with slatted wooden sides, through which the wine is pressed free of solid matter. It is now ready for its long schooling in the *crianza* or 'nursery', as it is appropriately called.

In the old bodegas numerous flights of steep stone steps lead down into an endless series of great subterranean chambers, occupied by vast oaken *tinas*, the vats used for secondary fermentation, in which the wine spends its first months, the huge oak barrels or *cuvas* to which it is later transferred, and finally the serried ranks of 225-litre *barricas* in which ageing is completed. At a bodega like Franco Españolas the *tinas* are eighty years old and of 30,000 litres capacity, while the *cuvas*, which hold 25,000 litres, are hardly less impressive. During this initial period a slow secondary fermentation continues with the throwing of a heavy sediment, and the wine is 'racked', i.e. decanted off the solids at the bottom of the container before being run into *barricas*, where in the case of the *reservas* it will be matured for years. Racking or transfer to fresh casks is thereafter carried out twice a year; nothing resembling a *solera* is used in the Rioja, but there is blending of different musts and, to a limited extent, of different vintages to even up the wine in poor years.

Of the many new wineries, which have come into existence as a result of a rising standard of living in Spain and an increased demand for better quality bottled wines, Bodegas Beronia are a good example. Of medium size with a capacity of 2 million litres and 4,000 oak *barricas*, the bodega is spotlessly clean and is in fact painted with an anti-cryptogrammic paint specially obtained from England. Fermentation takes place in 16 steel tanks coated with epoxy resin and with provision for water-cooling; the temperature is kept as close as possible to 21°C and is never allowed to rise above 25°C. The cement *depósitos* in which the new wine rests until being transferred to *barrica* have rounded corners to facilitate cleaning. The wines, a 5° año red and a red *reserva* spend 1½ to 2 years in *barrica* and two years or more in bottle; not surprisingly, Beronia is making first-rate wine. Another modern trend is to construct the buildings entirely above ground and to use fibre-glass insulation to obtain an even, cool temperature. Bodegas Muga in Haro age their wines in a building of this type – though using nothing but the traditional oak receptacles for making it – and certainly no one could complain of their wines, which have taken their place among the aristocrats from the Rioja since they first made a *clarete* in 1971 and a fuller-bodied 'Prado Enea' in 1970.

The final stages in the making of the wine are clarification and bottling. It is now compulsory to clear white wines by cooling them to a temperature at which potassium bitartrate is precipitated, and large steel refrigeration units are used for this purpose. For red wines the traditional method of 'fining' with beaten egg white to remove suspended matter and cloudiness, as practised at the Marqués de Riscal and elsewhere, is still the best. However, at bodegas like Santiago and Martínez Lacuesta even the red wine is clarified by refrigeration; and at Santiago the wine is pasteurised by exposure to infra-red radiation. The reader must judge by the results; wine is after all a living entity, and one of its fascinations is the subtle variation in flavour between one bottle and another.

By whatever method the wine is clarified, it is finally pumped into large vitreous-lined or stainless steel containers and thence to the *tren* or bottling line. A large bodega like Santiago can fill, cork, capsule and label 30,000 bottles an hour of either still or sparkling wine. *Reservas* made in small quantity are still sometimes bottled by hand from the *barrica* in traditional manner. In the past the wine, once bottled, was sold and sent out without delay, so that it depended for bottle age on the time that it had spent in the bins of a restaurant or middleman. The present trend, especially among the *bodegueros* of the new concerns, is to age the better wine in bottle for a further year.

BODEGAS AND WINES

Most of the larger bodegas of the Rioja Alta produce a range of wines: *tinto* and *clarete* of various ages and vintages; *blanco*, both dry, semi-sweet and sweet; and often a *rosado*. Bodegas Bilbainas even make a good sparkling wine, Royal Carlton, elaborated with all the care of Champagne in their deep underground cellars. The Rioja Alavesa makes mainly red wine with a high proportion of Tempranillo, sometimes as much as 90 per cent. As between these two sub-regions, the Alavesa wines tend to be big, fruity and soft (though some like those from Bodegas Alavesas are very light) and mature more rapidly than those from the Rioja Alta, which are brisker, fresher, more acid and last longer.

Spaniards habitually bracket the Riscal and Murrieta as among the best of red Riojas. Of the two, the Murrieta is a big, soft and oaky wine, while the Riscal (whose founder started the bodega in 1860 '*en la ilusión de elaborar un vino tinto al estilo de Burdeos*' ('with the idea of making a red wine in the style of Bordeaux') still contains a proportion of Cabernet Sauvignon and is in fact light, elegant and a little astringent in the manner of claret. The best reserves from both bodegas (e.g. the 1934 and 1960 'Castillo Ygay' from Murrieta and, for example, the 1922, 1958, 1964 and 1970 Riscal) are magnificent wines in their different fashion. Other red *reservas* and fine wines even by the standards of Bordeaux and Burgundy are CVNE's 'Imperial' and 'Viña Real'; La Rioja Alta's 'Reserva 904'; the 'Vendimia Especial' of Bodegas Bibainas; 'Prado Enea' from Muga; 'Cerro Añon' from Olarra; 'Monte Real' from Bodegas Riojanas; and the 'Bosconia' and 'Tondonia' *reservas* from that most traditional of all the bodegas, López de Heredia, which start somewhat hard and tannic, but mature gloriously.

Next in age and quality to the *reservas* comes a group of red wines usually about five years old. Among so many good and sound wines it is a little invidious to make recommendations, but as the reader is probably less familiar with them than clarets or Burgundies, a short list may help: Bilbainas' 'Viña Zaco'; the velvety 'Viña Ardanza' and lighter 'Viña Arana' from Bodegas La Rioja Alta; Paternina's fruity and full-bodied 'Viña Vial'; the full and soft 'Carta de Oro' from Berberana; the light and elegant *clarete* from Muga; the excellent reds from the Cooperativa de Labastida; the light and fragrant 'Solar de Samaniego' from Bodegas Alavesas; and the robust, but always very drinkable and reasonably priced 'Campo Viejo' from Savin.

Of the younger wines, the 4° año Murrieta and Riscal must come high on the list. Other very popular and less expensive 3° año and 4° año wines are: CUNE; Franco Españolas; 'Viña Pomal' and the lighter 'Viña Paceta' from Bilbainas; 'Viña Alberdi' from Bodegas La Rioja Alta (obtainable in the U.K. at Sainsburys); the well-made and attractively priced 'Cumbrero' from Montecillo; the superior 'Viña Salceda'; and the reds from the Marqués de Cáceres, less oaky than most and more in the French style. The enormously popular 'Banda Azul' from Paternina, which struck a bad patch after the transfer to the huge new modern bodega, is now very much its reliable and reasonably priced self.

The white Riojas are now of two types: the traditional white aged in oak and the lighter cold-fermented wines best drunk as young as possible. In Spain itself, perhaps the most popular wine of the first type is the 'Monopole' from CVNE, with its nice balance of oak and fruit. The white Murrieta is dry, but big and luscious, while the aristocrats of the older white Riojas are the Tondonias from López de Heredia, oaky, but not maderised and marvellously complete. It would be a great pity if wines such as these were to disappear in favour of the new-style lighter wines. Both have their place; and of the cold-fermented wines two of the best are the Marqués de Cáceres with its exceptionally fragrant nose and long-lasting fruity flavour, and the 'Faustino V' from Bodegas Faustino Martínez with an intriguing lemony finish. The white Riscal, pleasant as it is, is not a Rioja, but is made in Rueda (see below). Apart from these dry white wines, there are also sweet and semi-sweet varieties. One of my own favourites is the 'Diamante' from Franco Españolas with its dryish aftertaste.

Old Castile and León

Apart from the Rioja, the other wine-growing districts of Old Castile, the recently demarcated Ribera del Duero and Rueda and the undemarcated district of Toro, centre on the Duero valley and Valladolid. Valladolid is readily accessible from Madrid either by road or by fast electric train; from Logroño the most scenic route is by the N.111 to Soria. The road follows the gorges and forests of the Iregua River before climbing in a series of great sweeps to the 1,700 m Puerto de Piqueras; and either side of the summit there are breathtaking views of the wild Sierra de Urbión. Turn right at Soria and continue along the N.122 to Peñafiel. Convenient stopping places along the route are the Parador perched above Soria or the Albergue at Aranda de Duero. West of Aranda the road runs close to the river and passes the great mediaeval castle of Peñafiel islanded among the vineyards on its hump-backed hill.

RIBERA DEL DUERO

Among the best of the wines are those from Peñafiel made from the red *Tinto fino* (the Rioja Tempranillo) at the Cooperativa de Ribera del Duero, which ages its 'Protos' and *reservas* in oak in cellars tunnelled beneath the castle.

The vineyards of the famous Vega Sicilia are a further 15 km towards Valladolid and 40 km from the city. At this point the road runs down the centre of the Duero Valley, abruptly bounded on either side by low hills with outcrops of chalk, and through the middle of the estate and its vineyards, easily identifiable by roadside notices. The bodega, which perhaps more resembles a small Bordeaux château than any in Spain, is set back among trees between the road and the river; an introduction is essential if you wish to visit it. As already mentioned, its red wines (it produces no white) are quite exceptional and derive their qualities from the admixture of grapes originally brought from Bordeaux, the soil, and the exceptional care taken in making and maturing them.

The grapes are lightly crushed and transferred to cement vats where they are fermented for fifteen days. There is no pressing of the skins and pips which sink to the bottom of the vat at the end of the first fermentation, and only the must in the upper part of the vat is pumped into the *tinas*, the receptacles, made of American oak, used for secondary fermentation. Here the wine spends its first year, after which 225-litre *barricas* are employed. The wine is fermented and matured very slowly, and it is racked only once a year to avoid exposure to the atmosphere and acceleration of the ageing processes. Current production amounts to only 80,000 bottles a year, although plans are well-advanced for extending the vineyards and bodega to satisfy a demand which cannot at present be met. There are sufficient facilities for maturing only half the wine for the ten years minimum required if it is to be sold as Vega Sicilia; the remainder is bottled in its third or fifth year and sold as 'Valbuena'.

The bodega prints notes on vintages still available – at a price – in select restaurants, hotels and Paradors:

Reserva Especial. Soft, well-balanced and harmonious.
1953 Robust, agreeable acid, very aromatic.
1964 Soft, light acidity, very aromatic.
1966 Soft colour, delicate, aromatic.
1967 Light acidity, very delicate and smooth.

Valbuena
5° año Light acidity, smooth and forward nose.
3° año A little hard, agreeable colour.

Surprisingly enough considering its size, it is possible to eat very well in Peñafiel and to accompany the meal with a bottle of 'Valbuena' or the 'new' 1967 Vega Sicilia.

RUEDA AND TORO

The white wines of Rueda, both the traditional sherry-like type and the light, new-style wines, may be sampled in the bars and restaurants of Valladolid. If you wish to see the vineyards and bodegas, head south out of Valladolid by the C.610 to Serrada and La Seca, two of the main centres. The little town of Rueda itself, with the modern bodegas of the Marqués de Riscal on the outskirts, is on the N.6 a little further to the west. To visit Toro, famous of old for its sturdy red wines, continue northwards from Rueda along the N.6 to Tordesillas. Stop here to visit the Monastery of Santa Clara, with its remarkable Moorish patio and relics of the Emperor Charles V and his wife Juana la Loca, and continue another 33 km through the vineyards to the ancient town of Toro, with its Roman bridge, seignorial houses and mediaeval churches. By the side of the road you will see the tops of some of the underground *depósitos*, in which the wine is stored and into which the marauding French troops lowered themselves with ropes during the Peninsular War – to be met at knife-point by the proprietors.

There is an old refrain of one of the former rulers of León, which says a lot about the dark, full-bodied wine of Toro, known locally as *Sangre de Toro* or 'bull's blood':

> *Tengo un Toro que da vino y un León que se lo traga* .
> (I have a bull that gives wine and a lion that swills it)

LEÓN

The old city of León, at the centre of an increasingly important wine-producing area, lies 142 km north-west of Valladolid by the N.601. Its Gothic cathedral, with its flying buttresses and magnificent mediaeval glass, is among the finest in Spain; and to stay at the Hotel San Marcos, housed in a splendid sixteenth-century monastery, is an experience in itself.

All around the vineyards, situated mainly to the south of the city, you will see what appear at first sight to be prehistoric earthworks or giant ant-heaps. They are, in fact, peasant bodegas, still in use primitive though they are, dug deep into the ground, equipped with a beam press and a chimney to allow for the escape of carbon dioxide, and mounded over.

Centuries removed in its techniques is the large modern plant of VILE (Vinos de León) in León itself. Using modern continuous presses and cement vinification vats, it is this which makes the bulk of the León wines which have proved so popular abroad. They range from the young red and white 'Rey León' to older wines matured carefully in 225-litre oak *barrica*, such as the four-year-old 'Palacio de Guzmán' and the 'Don Suero' *reservas*.

Catalonia

The natural focus of the region, historically and geographically, is Barcelona, and if you arrive by air, hire a car and make this your centre. However, the wine-growing areas lie along a broad coastal belt from the French frontier to Priorato in the south, so that if coming by car from France you may conveniently progress from north to south. Cross the border by the motorway from Perpignan at Le Perthus. Continue through La Junquera to Figueras and turn left for Perelada, 6 km along the C.252. Visit the castle with its bodega and wine museum. Return to Figueras and continue along the N.11 or parallel motorway to Gerona. Visit the magnificent Gothic cathedral and proceed along the N.11 to Mataró. Just beyond Masnou, 14 km further on, turn right for Alella (if you wish to go by the A.17 motorway from Gerona, refer to Sheet 3 of the large-scale Firestone map). Inspect the vineyards and one of the bodegas in

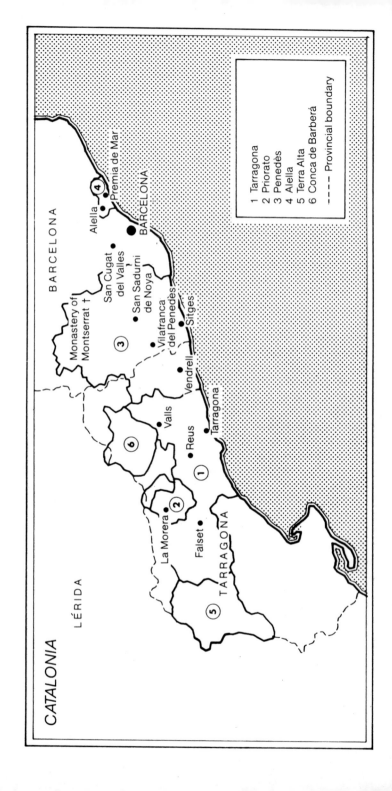

Alella, then take the motorway alternative of the N.11 into Barcelona. Stay at least one day to see the cathedral, the Museums of Catalan Art and Archaeology, to visit the Ramblas with their flower stalls and to eat at the harbour restaurants.

Head out of Barcelona by the road to the airport and continue along the coast by the C.246 to Sitges. Lunch there and sample the wine, then follow the tortuous but spectacular C.246 along the cliffs to Vendrell, where it joins the N.340 for Tarragona. Spend at least one night, allowing time to see the massive Roman walls and other remains, the fine mediaeval cathedral, the Chartreuse distillery and one or more of the great *bodegas de exportación*. If you wish to see the vineyards of Priorato, take the N.420 through Reus as far as Falset, some 50 km from Tarragona, then turn right up the winding mountain road, which will take you to Vilella and close to the ruins of the Monastery of Scala Dei, from which the wines took their name.

This side trip will hardly allow time on the same day for visits to Vilafranca del Penedès and San Sadurní de Noya, where there is a great deal to see. Start from Tarragona early for Vilafranca, some 50 km along the A.7 towards Barcelona. Visit the magnificent wine museum at Vilafranca, and also the Bodegas Torres, if arrangements can be made. Lunch in Vilafranca, or spend the night in the simple but adequate Hotel Pedro III El Grande, then take the C.243 to San Sadurní de Noya, 13 km away, to see the vast *cavas*, recently declared a National Monument, where Codorníu make their sparkling wines. From San Sadurní join the motorway, which will take you very quickly into Barcelona. If you are staying at one of the seaside resorts of the Costa Brava, it is also possible to make day excursions to these centres by taking advantage of the A.17 and other new motorways.

PERELADA

Perelada is best-known for its sparkling wine made in pressurised tanks by the *cuve-close* system, but also makes a good *cava* wine by the Champagne method, the 'Gran Claustro'. The cellars lie beneath the fourteenth-century church of Carmen de Perelada and the crenellated castle adjoining. The old buildings house a splendid library, a museum of glass and ceramics and an extensive wine museum, all open to the public. A more recent adjunct to the castle is a casino – but remember to bring a passport if you wish to chance your arm.

ALELLA

The best-known of the wines are made by the old-established Alella Vinícola (Bodegas Cooperativas). They are aged in oak for one or two years and none are sold before the three years required for the full development of flavour and bouquet. All the wine conforming to the *Denominación de Origen* is sold as 'Alella Legítima' and the Co-operative markets its produce under the trade mark 'Marfil' ('Ivory'). The white 'Marfil Blanco' is especially luscious, but on the sweet side to go with food other than desserts. There is a drier 'Marfil Seco', without quite the same roundness or fragrance, and also a light red 'Marfil Tinto' and a darker, more mature 'Supermarfil'. Alella also makes a rosé, an *Ojo de Gallo* ('partridge eye') and a sweet dessert wine, *Lacre Violeta*, well-matured, golden in colour, and unlike the others upwards of 14° in strength.

TARRAGONA

Tarragona is one of the most important centres in Spain for the manufacture of vermouths and liqueurs, described later (page 71). Apart from this it is largely given over to the blending and bulk export of inexpensive wines, some produced in the immediate region, but a great deal of which finds its way to the great *bodegas de exportación* from as far afield as La Mancha and Utiel-Requena. The bodegas line the dusty streets in the harbour area below the town proper. Typical examples are the Vinícola Iberica – from which a pipeline capable of delivering 150,000 litres an hour leads direct to the quayside – or de Muller down the road, a principal supplier of altar wines to the Vatican, and also the producer of a range of fine old *clássico* Tarragonas made in *solera*. The great sheds house rows of huge oak *tinas*, reminiscent of those in the Rioja, and underground *depósitos* of cement and stainless steel for storing and blending the wine; but the real heart of the establishments is the laboratory, where the chemists have perfected the art of matching samples sent to them by customers abroad. One of the big-selling exports is bottled *sangría*. This is best made fresh by adding ice-cubes, soda or 'fizzy lemonade', slices of orange and lemon and a dash of Spanish brandy to red wine; in response to the modern passion for 'convenience' products, it is made in Tarragona – and elsewhere in Spain – by mixing commercial citrus essence with the wine.

PRIORATO

Priorato is a small enclave in the much larger region of Tarragona. Its output of some 16,000 hectolitres annually is tiny. The red wines, dry, robust, inky black and high in alcohol, may be bought and drunk as such, but more often find their way to the bodegas of Tarragona for blending. Priorato also makes some good dessert wines from the Garnacho blanco, Macabeo and Pedro Ximénez grapes by cutting fermentation with the addition of alcohol. Wines like the golden *Blanco licoroso* and the *Rancio dulce* are so 'thick' as to cling to the glass and contain up to 20° of alcohol.

PENEDES

The Penedès area, extending from the Mediterranean coast to the heights of Montserrat some 700 metres up is the most varied and important of the Catalonian wine-growing regions.

Bajo Penedès, centring on the popular coastal resort of Sitges, is noted for its sweet wines, made from the Moscatel and Malvasía (Malmsey) grape, originally introduced from Greece or Cyprus and so inalienably connected with the unfortunate Duke of Clarence.

The main centres of wine-making in the Penedès are Vilafranca del Penedès and San Sadurní de Noya further north; and the best introduction to the regional wines is a visit to the wine museum at Vilafranca. Installed in a thirteenth-century palace of the kings of Aragón, this is one of the best of its kind in the world. It is not confined to the history of wine-making in Penedès or indeed of Spain as a whole, though there are extensive exhibits of *amphorae*, every type of wine-barrel and container, wine presses and models of bodegas of different periods from all parts of the country. Beyond this, there are tableaux illustrating the earliest known methods in Egypt, Greece and Rome. The visit ends in a small bar, where the local wine may be sampled and souvenirs may be bought – notably the *porrón*, of which Richard Ford wrote so picturesquely:

> They [the Catalans] often drink after the fashion of the Rhytium and phallo-citrobolic vessels of antiquity; they do not touch the glass with their lips, but hold up the *porrón*, or round-bellied bottle with a spout, at arm's length, pouring the cooled liquor into their mouths in a vinous parabola; they never miss the mark, while a stranger generally inundates his nose or his neckcloth.

The *porrón*, which may be of various sizes, is normally used in working-class households and in bars, when a group of friends are drinking together. Its advantage is that it dispenses with the need for glasses, since the spout never touches the lips. Unless you are skilled in its use, you may find it difficult to savour the wine from the thin jet that plays into the mouth and throat; tricks such as first running the wine down the nose are simply showmanship for the tourist.

The wine museum at Vilafranca, is not the only one of its kind in Spain, but it is the best arranged and most comprehensive. Drinking vessels such as the *porrón* and antique wine-making equipment may be seen in a variety of other places. Mention has already been made of the museum at Perelada (page 57), of the Bodega de San Ginés at Jerez (page

36) and of the exhibits at individual sherry bodegas; there is a charming small wine museum with interesting examples of old presses and vessels in the unlikeliest spot, the village of Villafamés in the hills behind Castellón de la Plana in the Levante, and the cellar of Chicote's famous bar in the Alcalá in Madrid houses a huge collection of curios and bottled wines from all over the world. Again, many local folk and archaeological museums possess interesting exhibits; a good example is that at Morella in the wild Maestrazgo up from Benicarló on the Levante coast, and it is always worthwhile going to such museums and, of course, those in larger places, to have a look.

There are numerous large firms in the Penedès making good quality table wines, both red and white. Among the best-known are René Barbier and the Conde de Caralt, both formerly within the RUMASA group; the Marqués de Monistrol, also known for its sparkling wines; Bodegas Bosch-Guell; and Masía Bach, with its great Florentine-style mansion, maker of big, fruity red wines and also the white 'Extrísimo', one of the most famous of Spanish dessert wines.

The largest and most prestigious of the firms is Bodegas Torres in Vilafranca del Penedès, which ships its wines all over the world – annual sales in the USA have recently topped a million bottles. Under its President, Don Miguel Torres Carbó, it is very much of a family concern; and his son, also Miguel Torres, one of the most outstanding oenologists in Europe, has been responsible for a bold new venture – the acclimatisation of noble foreign varieties of vine in the Penedès.

The wines are fermented in temperature-controlled stainless steel tanks, and Torres was a pioneer in Spain of making white wines by 'cold fermentation' and of bottling them without maturation in oak. Typical of these are the various styles of the dry, fresh and fruity 'Viña Sol', 'Gran Viña Sol' and the semi-dry 'Esmeralda', made with a blend of acclimatised Gewürztraminer and Moscatel d'Alsace. The red wines spend 1½ to 2 years in cask and more time in bottle than most from the Rioja, and are therefore less oaky. Some, like the fruity and full-bodied 'Tres Torres' and 'Gran Sangre de Toro', are made from native grapes; the superior 'Magdala' contains Pinot Noir; while the pride of the Torres stable, the beautiful 'Gran Coronas Black Label', winner of so many international awards, is made from Cabernet Sauvignon and Cabernet Franc.

Torres welcomes visitors to its bodega, and one feature which always arouses interest is the large pear-shaped demi-johns in serried ranks, left out in the patio and used for making a white *vino rancio*. The *bombonas* in effect form a simple open-air *solera*, and the end-product is agreeably sherry-like in taste.

Ninety per cent of all Spanish *cava* or sparkling wine is made in the Penedès region; and the centre of the industry is the neighbouring town of San Sadurní de Noya. Its manufacture by the Champagne method was first begun in 1872 by Don José Raventós, whose family firm of Codorníu had been making still wines in the area since 1551. Apart from the vast *cavas* of Codorníu, San Sadurní is also the headquarters for numerous other firms such as Freixenet, Segura Viudas, Monistrol, Castellblanch and Gonzalez y Dubosc – to mention only a few of the best-known.

Once inside one of the *cavas*, with its endless subterranean network of chilly, dripping vaults and passages, it is difficult to realise that you are not at Rheims, since the methods, although not the grapes, are exactly the same as those of the French Champagne firms.

Most of these sparkling wines correspond to a French *blanc de blancs* in being made only from white grapes, chiefly the Xarello, imparting alcoholic strength and colour; the Macabeo (or Viura), contributing finesse and elegance; and the Parellada from the hill slopes, with its fresh and fruity nose. Smaller amounts of pink wine are made by admixing a little black Cariñena or Garnacho tinto.

Fermentation is no longer carried out in barrels, but in stainless steel tanks at low temperature so as to conserve the aroma and taste of fruit. At Freixenet these tanks are truly enormous, with a capacity of 600,000 litres. Once the wine has settled, it is cooled to $-0.4°C$ to precipitate tartrate and there now follows the process which distinguishes sparkling wines of this type from all others. Prior to bottling in the characteristic thick 800 ml bottles, capable of sustaining a pressure of six atmospheres, a calculated amount of cane sugar dissolved in old wine is added. The bottles are now securely closed with temporary corks secured by metal *grapas* (hooks) or with the more modern crown caps; and under the action of cultivated yeasts the sugar is very slowly converted to carbon dioxide gas and alcohol. The quality of a good sparkling wine with long-lasting bubbles is dependent on carrying out this fermentation extremely slowly at a low temperature over a period of three to four years – hence the necessity for cool underground vaults and the inferiority of wines made more rapidly at higher temperatures.

The trickiest part of the whole process is the removal of the sediment which forms in the bottle over this period, and it is accomplished by very gradually, over a period of six months, inverting the bottle in an adjustable wooden frame known as a *pupitre*. The Catalan *cavas* have more recently introduced *girasols* (or 'sunflowers'), metal frames on a faceted base holding some 500 bottles, which achieve the same result with a great deal less labour. The most dramatic moment in any visit to a cellar of this sort is the deft removal of the temporary cork and the ejection of the sediment – sometimes the neck of the bottle is frozen, so that the pressure of gas expels it in a solid plug. In case of accidents it is advisable not to stand too near the operator, on pain of being christened like a newly launched ship! After topping up with a brandied *licor de expedición* the wine is now ready for re-corking, capping and wiring.

In increase order of sweetness Spanish *espumosos*, which can be of excellent quality, are labelled:

> **Natur, Brut, Bruto.** Dry.
> **Seco.** Fairly dry.
> **Semiseco.** Semi-dry.
> **Semidulce.** Semi-sweet.
> **Dulce.** Sweet.

Before leaving San Sadurní de Noya it is highly instructive to visit a completely different type of establishment, the great Cooperativa Vinícola of Penedès. Wine writers can easily convey a false impression by describing only the best of what a country or region produces. As in France, Italy and Portugal, the co-operatives perform an essential function by buying grapes from the local farmers and in making the bulk of wine for everyday consumption. In Spain, much of the co-operative wine is well-made, and is in fact bought and matured in private bodegas to be sold under their label – a practice even more common in areas of Portugal like the Dão and Vinhos Verdes. The co-operative at San Sadurní is of particular interest as being one of the most modern in Spain, with a capacity of twelve million litres, and serves as a reminder that the wines which have been described form only a drop in the ocean of the four million hectolitres produced each year in Catalonia.

Aragón and Navarra

These areas, of relatively minor importance, may conveniently be visited if you are driving from Barcelona to Logroño and the Rioja. Take the A.7 and A.2 motorways through Lérida to Saragossa, 300 km to the west of Barcelona, and leave by the N.330 for Cariñena 47 km to the south. Inspect the vineyards and bodegas, then return to Saragossa and head north-west by the A.68 motorway for Tudela, the main centre for the wines of the Ribera Baja of southern Navarra. Then, 14 km beyond Tudela, turn right up the N.121 or parallel A.15 motorway for Pamplona. The best Navarra wines are made in Las Campanas, 16 km short of Pamplona, and Puente La Reina 12 km west, at the junction of the side road from Las Campanas and the N.111 from Pamplona to Logroño. A very pleasant place to stay is at the Parador installed in the historic old castle of the kings of Navarra at Olite, which offers a selection of the regional wines.

Writing in the early nineteenth century, the great Spanish authority, Simon de Roxas Clemente, rated Cariñena as the most delicate of Spanish wines; today the district is better known as a large reservoir of pleasant wines for everyday drinking. Traditionally, they were fermented in underground stone cisterns, but are now mostly made in the cement-lined tanks of the large co-operatives, of which the Cooperativa San Valero in Cariñena itself is one of the best-known. The typical wines are the big red *tintos* and *claretes*, much used for blending as well as for direct consumption, because of their high alcoholic strength, which may approach 18°.

Tudela, on the Ebro, produces robust wines after the style of the neighbouring Rioja Baja; of more style and character are those from the Vinícola Navarra at Las Campanas. The 'Clarete Campanas' is dry, soft and bordering on a rosé, while the 'Castilo de Tiebas 5° año', available in the U.K., is full-bodied, fruity and mature, and a very good buy.

It is certainly worth paying a visit to the Señorio de Sarriá (H. Beaumont y Cía.) near Puente de la Reina, on the old pilgrim route to Santiago; but this will present difficulties unless you can get in touch with the management and make arrangements beforehand, since the beautiful domaine, which embraces a castle, orchards and a stock-raising establishment, as well as vineyards and a model winery, is as carefully supervised as any estate in California, and the approach is by a gatehouse where a uniformed security guard scrutinises credentials.

Production under carefully regulated conditions has been under way only since 1952, but the winery was extended in 1959 and now has a capacity of six thousand 225 *barricas*, made in the bodega's own coopery from Armagnac oak, for maturing its wine, some of which is now exported. The youngest of the red wines is the sound three-year-old 'Ecoyen'; there is a more mature and very smooth and fruity 'Viña del Perdón' of some 13° strength and also excellent old 'Gran Vino del Señorio de Sarría' *reservas*. All of these wines are made from the same grapes as Riojas (Tempranillo, Mazuelo, Graciano and Garnacho), and the bodega also grows a little Cabernet Sauvignon in its very extensive vineyards. Francisco Moriones, its highly expert oenologist, considers that his best recent vintages were 1964, 1970, 1973, 1975 and 1978. All the wines which include whites and a rosé, may be sampled at good hotels in Pamplona or in the Parador at Olite.

Galicia

The mountainous north-west of Spain is the most difficult of access of any part of the country. The best times for a visit are the early summer, when its granite-strewn heights resemble a vast rock garden flamboyant with yellow broom and studded with mountain flowers, or at the time of the grape harvest in September. During the late autumn, winter and spring, it tends to be uniformly wet.

There are overnight trains from Madrid to Vigo and points north; if you are coming by car, the most direct approach is by the ferry to Santander. Take the N.634 west – it is worth by-passing Oviedo and lunching at the really excellent restaurant of the Parador at Gijón – and continue along the coast through the apple orchards of Asturias by the N.632 and N.634. This route, between mountains and sea, skirting the romantic but disused narrow-gauge railway, is one of the most beautiful in Spain, but far from fast. One or other of the Paradors, at Ribadeo on the coast or Villalba in the mountains inland, is probably as far as you can comfortably manage in a day. From Villalba, continue along the N.634 and turn right when it joins the main N.6 for La Coruña. Five km beyond Guitíriz, turn left on to the C.544 and follow it down through the pine and eucalyptus to Santiago de Compostela.

Break your journey to visit the cathedral and shrine of St. James (the Hotel Reyes Católicos is one of the most magnificent in Spain), then head south along the N.550, where for the first time you will be in wine country and can see the vines strung high between granite pillars. At Puentecesures branch right on to the C.55 and follow it along the shores and sparkling blue waters of the Ría de Arosa to Cambados. Spend the night at the Parador, inspect the Palace of Fefiñanes and sample its Albariño wine. Continue south along the coast by the C.550 to Pontevedra, join the N.550 and continue south as far as Porriño. If you want to investigate the wines of the Condado de Salvatierra, spend a night at Tuy or Bayona (consult Sheet 1 of the large-scale Firestone map – a few nights at the splendid sea-girt Parador of Bayona are in themselves worth the long journey from Santander).

From Porriño, take the N.120 to visit Ribadavia and its co-operative, the largest in Galicia, which lie below the main road in the valley of the Miño approximately two-thirds of the way to Orense. From Orense you may continue 100 km along the N.120 to El Barco de Valdeorras or strike south-east down the N.525 to Verín, where there is a comfortable Parador near the vineyards of Monterrey. Both places make wines of repute, but Valdeorras is one of the most inaccessible spots in a far-flung region; and from Verín (or much more easily from Tuy) you may cross into Portugal for a very instructive comparison of its *vinhos verdes* with the *pétillant* Galician wines.

In both areas you will see the same method of growing the vines by training them well clear of the ground from granite posts or chestnut stakes; indeed there is a saying in Galicia:

> *Quien no tiene madera, no tiene viña*
> (He who has no wood has no vineyard)

As in the Portuguese Minho, the reason is both to keep the grapes clear of the damp ground and also to minimise exposure to reflected sunshine, since the excess acid in the partially ripe fruit is afterwards broken down during a secondary malo-lactic fermentation. To avoid repetition, the special method of fermentation will be described later in connection with the better-known Portuguese *vinhos verdes* (page 108). What is astonishing is the almost entire ignorance of wine writers – there are of course honourable exceptions – as to the very existence of the delightful 'green wines' of Galicia. The explanation may be that very little has been exported to England since the Methuen Treaty of 1703, and when these wines were made in peasant bodegas they often suffered from turbidity and would not travel. This is certainly no longer the case since the co-operatives introduced refrigeration plant for clarifying and stabilising them.

As in the Portuguese *vinho verde* area, considerably more red wine is produced than white; the wines vary from those with a definite slight bubble to others which leave only a prickling sensation on the tongue and are usually drunk young at any time after the late spring following the harvest.

The best of the Galician wines, the white Albariños, may be tasted in their variety at the Fiesta del Albariño, held at Cambados in mid-August. Like its famous counterpart, the Alvarinho from Monção, just over the border, the renowned 'Fefiñanes Palacio', made by the Marqués de Figueroa in the palace on the outskirts of the town, is hardly a *vino verde* proper, since the *reservas* undergo ageing of up to six years in oak casks, by which time they emerge golden in colour, more fully flavoured and less acid than the typical *pétillant* growths of the district, pale in colour, delicate, dry and fruity. A good example is the 'Albariño del Palacio', made by the Marquis' brother.

The Condado de Salvatierra makes good wines, typically *pétillant* and both red and white, but the difficulty is to find them, since the district is small and none are bottled on a commercial scale. The largest producer of Galician wine is the district in the extreme south-west of the Province of Orense. The area centres on the township of Ribadavia and the confluence of the Sil and Miño Rivers – further west the Miño forms the frontier with Portugal and marks the northern limit of the *vinho verde* area. Of the 250,000 hectolitres of wine produced annually, the most attractive is the white, well-balanced, fresh, fairly acid, and of 10° to 12° strength with a slight sparkle. The wines which you will most frequently encounter in Spanish hotels and restaurants are those from the Bodega Cooperativa de Ribeiro, which will travel well thanks to modern methods of stabilisation and refrigeration. In addition to producing *aguardiente* (*marc*), the co-operative makes seven types of wine:

Blanco	Pazo
	LAR
	Xeito
	Granel (bulk)
Rosado	Pazo
Tinto	Pazo
	Xeito

In each category the 'Pazo', which takes its name from a word meaning a baronial residence, is the best. The white 'Pazo' is practically without sparkle; the *rosado* is more definitely a *pétillant* wine, a tendency even more pronounced in the uncompromising red wines, which are dry to the point of acidity. It is traditional in Galicia to drink the fuller-bodied red wines in shallow bowls, about four inches in diameter and made of glazed white earthenware, so as to set off their deep ruby colour. These are obtainable at the Cooperativa and are sometimes used in Galician restaurants such as El Mesón Gallego in the Calle Leganitos, near the Plaza de España in Madrid.

In the valley of the Tamega around Verín and Monterrey the vines are pruned low and grown without support *a la castellana* and produce strong red wines of up to 14° strength. Here, as in Valdeorras to the north, which also makes sound wines both red and white, they are sometimes without the *pétillance* so typical of the others. A first-rate example is the still white Valdeorras *blanco* of the Cooperativa El Barco available from Laymont and Shaw of Falmouth, who have done much to popularise Spanish regional wines in England.

Extremadura

The Extremadura produces some unusual wines made in small bodegas as well as a great deal of *vino comun* from the district around Almendralejo, but it is hardly worth making a special journey unless you wish to combine it with visits to the remarkable Roman remains in Mérida or the splendid

Monastery of Guadalupe. The best centre is Mérida, 343 km west of Madrid along the fast N.5 or 227 km from Lisbon by way of the N.4 in Portugal and N.5 over the border in Spain.

To visit Guadalupe, follow the N.5 from Madrid through the dusty outskirts of Talavera le Reina, well known for its tiles and ceramics, as far as Oropesa. Turn left into the spectacular mountain road, which climbs to the 807 m Puerto de San Vicente, then drops down into Guadalupe. Stay the night at the Parador, visit the historic monastery, with its beautiful Zurbarán paintings and remarkable collections of jewelled vestments and mediaeval psalters, and sample the white *flor*-growing wine of Canamero. They will be pleased enough to show you the wine, slowly bubbling under its layer of *flor* in any of the small bodegas of the village, 17 km further on towards Mérida along the C.401. Continue through Logrosán until you rejoin the main N.5.

Stay at the Parador in Mérida and allow a day or two to explore the splendid Roman Theatre, amphitheatre, aqueduct, triumphal arch and remains of villas and tesselated pavements, and also to make side trips to the villages and townships around. Some of the local red wines and *claretes* are highly individual and can only be drunk on the spot.

Montánchez, 70 km north by the N.5 towards Madrid and then by the C.520 branching off to the left into a rolling sierra dotted with cork oak, makes what must be one of the few *red* wines to grow a *flor*. Deep orange in colour and slightly turbid, it is certainly worth tasting if only for its unusual pedigree.

The road south from Mérida passes through Almendralejo, which produces a vast amount of wine, both red and white, for everyday drinking. Nineteen km further on, a turning to the right at Los Santos leads through Zafra, the site of a magnificent castle, now a Parador, beyond which lies Salvatierra de los Barros, whose red wine, aromatic, brilliant and intensely coloured is appreciated by cognoscenti as far afield as Madrid.

Both Trujillo and Medellín, the birthplaces of the Conquistadores Cortés and Pizarro, make wines of some repute. Both are within easy driving distance of Mérida; and Trujillo in particular, with its fine arcaded square and castle, is well worth a visit. The wine from Medellín, red, white and rosé, is made in a large modern bodega on the outskirts of the town and bottled under the label 'Castello de Medellín'. It may be sampled at the Parador in Mérida.

New Castile and the Levante

The vast and arid central plateau of Spain and the southern hinterland of the Mediterranean produce an enormous volume of wine, both red and white, most of it for everyday drinking or shipment abroad and to other parts of Spain for blending. Certain wines stand out, like the best from Valdepeñas and Utiel-Requena, but it would not be practical to attempt a comprehensive tour of this huge area, unless you have weeks, rather than days, to spare. Most of the wine is made in the cement tanks of the co-operatives – and one co-operative is very like another. The suggested itinerary, covering some of the more important centres, will give a good enough general impression.

Start either from Madrid or Valencia – if you fly direct, a car may be hired in either place. From Madrid, take the N.4 south and stop in Aranjuez to see the palace and its beautiful gardens. The road now continues through Don Quixote country, with the occasional clustered windmills and sunbaked white villages. At Puerto Lápice, where the balconied inn mentioned by Cervantes has been done up and is still open, turn left on the N.420 for Alcázar de San Juan and here turn right along the C.400 for Tomelloso. Both townships are centres for distilling grape spirit, much of it sent to Jerez de la Frontera for making brandy. Alcázar specialises in the manufacture of vinegar and *arrope vínico*, a syrup made by evaporating and concentrating unfermented must, used in making sweet dessert wines and vermouths and also sold to do-it-yourself wine-making clubs abroad. As one of its manufacturers remarked expansively, 'It doesn't make very good wine, but it's delicious spread on bread and butter!' Various concerns in Tomelloso also produce anis and liqueurs.

Turn right along the C.310 at Tomelloso, rejoining the N.4 near Manzanares, where the Parador de Manzanares is a convenient stopover. Continue along the N.4 to Valdepeñas, on a bumpy diversion off the main road, the most important wine centre of the entire region. Cut across country by the C.415 to Alcarez, then follow the N.322 and N.430 through Albacete to Almansa, dominated by one of the most spectacular castles in Spain. If you wish to drink the powerful black wine of Yecla on the spot, make a side trip along the mountainous C.323 to visit the well-known Cooperativa Agricola la Purisima at Yecla, 31 km to the south. From Almansa continue along the N.430 to Valencia. Spend a night or two; there is plenty to see – do not miss the splendid ceramic museum in the Palace of the Marqués de Dos Aguas – and the regional wines may be sampled in the numerous bars and cafés. Head out by the main N.3 for Madrid, which will take you through the important wine towns of Requena and Utiel.

Devotees of anisette may care to make the short diversion to Chinchón, where the best-known Spanish brand of the same name is produced. Turn left at Villarejo de Salvanés, 49 km short of Madrid. The road follows through the picturesque old town, rejoining the N.3 via the C.300. It was a seventeenth-century Marquesa de Chinchón, wife of a governor of Peru, who gave her name to quinine. About 1638 she used an extract from the bark of the evergreen tree, subsequently called the Cinchona, to cure a fever. Specimens were thereafter taken by the Spanish priests to Europe, where it was first known as 'Jesuits' Bark'.

Of all the wines from this huge area, Valdepeñas is the most noteworthy. The traditional method of fermenting and maturing it is in ten foot-high earthenware *tinajas*, still to be seen in the bodegas of the town – though in the larger establishments they are giving way to the ubiquitous cement *depósitos*. The wine is normally drunk young and often sold from the *tinaja* during the spring following the vintage. It may, however, be shipped to other parts of Spain and matured in oak; some of the better white Valdepeñas was formerly sent north for 'education' and blending with the cheaper white Riojas. There are certain favoured vineyards, such as those of Los Llanos to the west of the town and Las Aberturas to the north; but it is usually impossible to identify the source and the wine is most often served from a carafe. The town's commercial 'wine museums' (containing little except serried ranks of bottles) offer a bewildering variety of different marks; but it is profitless to pay too much attention to names and labels. Valdepeñas celebrates a *Fiesta de la Poesía y Vendimia* on 3 September, a literary event in praise of Manchegan wines.

Without leaving Madrid and at very little expense, you may drink excellent house Valdepeñas in the restaurants and old-fashioned tiled bars in streets such as Ventura de la Vega and Echegaray near the Puerta del Sol in the old city. Fresh, fruity and supple, with excellent bouquet, they are paragons of good carafe wines.

The best of the Levante wines are the rosés from Utiel-Requena. The provinces of Alicante and Murcia, to the south of Valencia, and Castellón, to the north, all produce wine in plenty, as does Valencia itself. Whether red or white, they tend to be 'earthy' and heavy with an excessive content of alcohol – though no-one could say that they are anonymous or lack character.

Balearics

The Balearics, comprising Majorca, Minorca and the smaller islands of Ibiza and Formentera, do not, I think, merit a special visit to taste their wines. Much is imported in bulk from the mainland and simply bottled on the spot. Sixty per cent of the local production, mainly of red *corriente*, is from the vineyards of

Binisalem, Felanitx and Manacor in Majorca, served by various co-operatives, the largest at Felanitx. But if on holiday in Majorca, do not fail to ask for the wine made by a wealthy connoisseur, José L. Ferrer, on his estate at Binisalem, near Inca north of the capital. Mostly red, it is made from the local Montenegro grape; the bodega produces a young and very fresh 'Auténtico' and also excellent full-bodied *reservas*, which should be tasted on the spot, since production is too limited for their export in any quantity.

Spirits, Aromatic Wines and Liqueurs

BRANDY

Surprisingly enough, brandy, often known as *coñac*, is both cheaper and more popular in Spain than sherry. The bulk of it is not, however, made like cognac by the distillation of locally grown grapes in small pot stills. The grapes used in Spain are those surplus to the production of table wine from widely scattered areas of the country, and the original distillation of the wine and subsequent *elaboración* are not normally carried out in the same establishment. The starting point for Spanish brandy is a 65 per cent grape spirit or *holandas* produced in the large continuous stills of a place like Tomelloso (see page 68), although some firms, like Pedro Domecq, do maintain distilleries of their own, though not at Jerez de la Frontera, where most of the brandy is elaborated and matured. The crude *holandas* are redistilled, a fraction containing impotable methyl alcohol is rejected, and the spirit is diluted to about 45 per cent. Flavouring extracts are often added; and the raw brandy is then set aside to mature in old sherry butts of American oak and aged in a *solera*, the mature brandy being drawn off and the *solera* 'refreshed' with younger from a *criadera* as in the manufacture of sherry.

The cheaper Spanish brandies are generally darker, less fragrant and less delicate than their French counterparts, and some, like the ordinary 'Terry' and 'Osborne', are somewhat sweet and caramelised. The large-selling 'Soberano' and 'Fundador' are distinctly drier. There are other more delicate and refined Spanish brandies made like cognac by a double distillation in Charentais-type stills. Among these are the soft and fragrant (and very expensive) 'Lepanto' from Gonzalez Byass and the lighter and somewhat sweeter 'Carlos I' from Pedro Domecq. Both of these are Jerez brandies matured in *solera*; but there are also excellent Catalan brandies matured like those from Cognac and Armagnac, and less oaky in style. Of these, the best are the Miguel Torres 'Black Label' and the 'Don Narciso' from Antonio Mascaró, whose regular

'Mascaró' is in my own opinion much superior to most 3-star cognacs and a great deal less expensive.

AGUARDIENTE

Another very popular spirit in Spain is the water-white *aguardiente*, which by definition covers the liquor distilled from vegetable material of any type – grapes, other fruit, potatoes, and stalks – including the 'D.Y.C.' whisky made near Segovia and the rather more satisfactory Larios gin from Málaga. However, over the counter of a bar, *aguardiente* means *arguardiente de orujo*, or colloquially *orujo*, made by distilling grape skins and pips in the manner of the French *marc* or Portuguese *bagaceira*. In Galicia they prepare a deceptively mild *queimada* by pouring the spirit into an earthenware *cazuela*, adding roasted coffee beans, slices of fresh lemon and maraschino cherries and then setting alight the fiery concoction and burning off some of the alcohol, and a simpler *queimada* is made by setting fire to a little *aguardiente* in one of the small bowls used for drinking red wine (see page 66); when the blue flame dies down the liquid is left almost cold. In the words of the *cooperativistas* of Ribeiro, it is a drink which 'requires three men to a glass: one to drink it and two friends to support him'. A further form of *aguardiente* is the anis from Chinchón, made by blending grape spirit with an extract of aniseed in alcohol and excellent of its kind.

VERMOUTH AND OTHER APÉRITIFS

Although Italy and France have a virtual monopoly of the international market for vermouth and aromatic wines, large quantities are made in Spain to supply domestic needs and for export to South America. Whatever the final style of the vermouth, the basis is a fortified white wine flavoured with a complex extract of herbs. The darker, sweeter varieties contain sugar or *mistela* (sugary must in which fermentation has been arrested by addition of alcohol) and also caramel. The prime requirements are therefore an abundant supply of cheap white wine and a good recipe; and the Cinzano and Martini made under licence in Vilafranca del Penedès and Barcelona are virtually indistinguishable from their Italian namesakes. Other well-known apéritif wines, such as Dubonnet, Ricard and Amer Picon, are also produced in Spain, the main centres of manufacture being Barcelona, Tarragona, Reus and Tomelloso.

VINOS QUINADOS AND OTHER DRINKS

More typically Spanish are the *Vinos Quinados* or medicated wines, of which the best-known is 'Jerez-Quina', made by macerating cinchona bark and the skins of bitter Seville oranges in sugared white wine or a blend of sherry and *mistela*. Quinine is also used for making that bitterest of apéritifs, Calisay.

Like vermouths, many of the best-known liqueurs (*licores*) are made under licence in Spain, where they are very cheap. Since the flavour and aroma depend much more on the blend of herbs and method of fabrication than on the alcohol base, there is again little to choose between the original and the Spanish version. On this basis, Cointreau is made at Vilafranca del Penedès, Bénédictine in Madrid, and Marie Brizard at Pasajes in the Basque country.

A monk in the Chartreuse cellars at Tarragona

Chartreuse is more closely linked with Spain. In 1903 the anti-clerical policies of the French Government resulted in the expropriation of the Carthusians from their monastery at Fauvoirie, and the fathers set up a large distillery in Tarragona, which was the sole producer of the liqueur until their return to Grenoble in 1940. Yellow and green Chartreuse and also the 'Elixir' are now made both at a new distillery at Voiron and in Tarragona, the three monks who share the secret dividing their time between the two establishments. Visitors are welcome at the Tarragona distillery, which is built around a cool courtyard planted with palm trees and fragrant with the smell of herbs; no prior arrangements are necessary, other than checking the times of opening at your hotel. The visit ends with a tasting in an arched *salón de degustación*, which features a collection, running to scores of bottles, of fraudulent imitations.

6

Regional Cooking

Spanish cooking is as varied as the wines and is firmly based on the wide variety of fresh ingredients available in the different regions of the country. It is of interest that many of the essential elements of modern cooking were first introduced to France and Western Europe by way of Spain. The staples of Mediterranean cooking, olive oil and garlic, were first brought to the area by the Romans who colonised Spain; oranges, lemons, sugar cane, saffron and a variety of spices were introduced by the Moors; and the Conquistadors returned from America in the seventeenth century, not only with gold and silver, but potatoes, tomatoes, pimientos and chocolate. A major contribution was the invention of mayonnaise, of which the recipe was taken to France from Port Mahón in Minorca (the name is derived from Mahón) by Cardinal Richelieu (1585–1642).

The Ministry of Tourism publishes a gastronomic map, reproduced in its brochure *Gastronomía España*, obtainable free in its many local offices in Spain or in the Paradors and Albergues; it indicates the broad characteristics of the regions. Andalusia is labelled the *Zona de Fritos* (fried foods); Valencia and the Levante, the *Zona de Arroces* (rice); the Castiles, the *Zona de los Asados* (roasts); Aragon and Navarra, the *Zona de los Chilindrones* (piquant sauces made from tomatoes and peppers); Catalonia, the *Zona de Pescados* (fish); and the north coast, the *Zona de las Salsas* (sauces).

Andalusia and Extremadura

One of the best ways of starting a meal in Andalusia and the Extremadura, so relentlessly hot in summer, is with one of the variants of the cold *Gazpacho,* an ice-cold soup made from a variety of uncooked vegetables, often chopped or ground in a mortar, and always containing olive oil, vinegar and garlic; an alternative to the familiar version made with tomatoes and peppers is the *Ajo blanco con uvas* from Málaga, a blend of garlic and ground almonds served ice-cold with fresh grapes floating in it.

Typical of the fried dishes is the *Fritura mixta de pescados*, containing inkfish, fresh sardines and anchovies, and in terms of fish, corresponding to a mixed grill; it goes excellently with cold

Montilla or with one of the sherry-flavoured wines such as Chiclana. The Extremadura is famous for its *jamón serrano,* a dark, highly cured ham, after the style of Parma or Bayonne ham, but even more intense in flavour. It is made by impregnating a fresh leg of pork with coarse salt, marinating it in white wine over a period of months, coating it with a paste of sweet paprika and olive oil and hanging it up to dry over a further period of months; in some regions *jamón serrano* is further cured by burying it in the snow. Sliced wafer thin, it is eaten as a starter, with or without the luscious melon from the district, and is obtainable all over the country. The best of these hams, which are used in a variety of egg and vegetable dishes, are from Montánchez, also noted for its wines, and Jabugo.

Throughout the south of Spain there is a variety of local sweetmeats, Moorish in origin, but later made by the nuns in their convents, often from almonds and eggs.

Valencia and the Levante

Valencia and the Levante are best-known for *paella.* This saffron-tinted rice dish may be made simply with fish, when it is called a *paella marinera,* or with chicken, meat and small sausages. It is now so popular all over the country that it might almost be called the national dish and is cooked to perfection along the Basque coast with the abundant local shellfish. The Spaniards *always* accompany *paella* with a full-bodied red wine – and rightly because white wine does not usually stand up to its full flavour. The heavy Levante wines are incidentally acceptable enough on a picnic, which in Spain usually consists of a thick slice of cold *tortilla* (Spanish omelette) – those containing onion as well as potato are the juicier – or a *bocadillo* made by sandwiching Manchego cheese or the highly spiced *chorizo* sausage in the excellent crusty bread. The best *chorizo* for a cold meal is that from Pamplone; those from Salamanca are used to advantage in the rib-warming *cocidos* (or vegetable stews) from the north.

Old Castile

Some of the best dishes from Old Castile (north of Madrid) are the roasts of lamb, pork and kid. Segovia and Avila are famous for their *Cochinillo* or sucking pig, which, after roasting in a baker's oven, is so tender that it may be cut with a plate. Equally delicious is the *Lechazo,* roasted milk-fed lamb, unobtainable in England where it is forbidden to kill the lambs at such an early age. This is at its best around Valladolid, and at Haro and Logroño in the Rioja, where the ideal accompaniment is a good vintage *tinto* or *clarete.* Traditional fare during the bitter Castilian winter is *Cocido castellano,* a rich meat stew made with chick peas and a variety of other vegetables and served on separate plates as soup, vegetable and meat. It goes well with a red Valdepeñas.

Aragón and Navarra

The peppery Chilindrón sauce from Aragon and Navarra is often served with chicken (*Pollo al chilindrón*); a cooling dry white Rioja or Navarra wine is suitably refreshing. *Trucha a la Navarra* fried trout opened and sometimes sandwiched with *jamón serrano*, also calls for a dry white wine.

Catalonia was known for the variety of its cuisine even before 1477, when Maestre Rupert de Nola published his *Llibre de Coch*, one of the first cookery books to appear in Europe. For some hundred-and-fifty years from the beginning of the twelfth century the Languedoc and Provence were dominated by the Counts of Barcelona, and it seems entirely likely that such present-day Provençal favourites such as *aioli* (or in its Catalan form, *ali-oli*), *bouillabaisse* and *cassoulet*, all of which were popular in Catalonia from a very early date, were introduced to the region from over the Pyrenees. Today the seafood may be eaten at its best in the restaurants clustering around the harbour at Barcelona.

One famous Catalan dish is *Zarzuela,* which takes its name from the Spanish word for a 'variety show', and indeed consists of a variety of shellfish and firm whitefish in a rich sauce containing tomatoes and onions. A particularly delicious sweet is the *Crema quemada a la catalana,* a baked custard topped with the thinnest film of brittle caramel.

The Basque Country

The Basque region to the north is also exceptional for the variety of fish from the colder waters of the Atlantic. Take your choice from the great assortment of excellent fish dishes: *Merluza a la vasca* (Basque style hake); *Sardinas fritas* (fried fresh sardines); *Calamares en su tinta* (baby squid in their ink); *Mejillones a la marinera* (*moules marinières*); *Angulas* (tiny freshwater eels); *Kokotxas* (strips cut from the throat of the hake); *Gambas al piz pil* (fried prawns in chilli sauce); or *Bacalao a la viscaina* (a classic way of preparing the dried salted cod, so popular in Spain and Portugal). Although it is difficult to find it in sophisticated restaurants, the *pétillant* Chacolí wine is a piquant companion to fish, especially *mariscos* (shellfish).

Continuing westwards along the Atlantic, the mountains lying back from the coast abound in game. A particularly intriguing combination is stewed partridge with a bitter chocolate sauce (*Perdices estofadas a la catalana*). The most famous dish of the region is *Fabada asturiana,* another nourishing stew, particularly welcome during the long wet winter, and containing broad beans, brisket of beef and *morcilla asturiana* (a type of black pudding). This, of course, calls for a full-bodied *tinto*.

Galicia

Galicia in the far north-west is gastronomically one of the richest regions of the whole country and its cooking has many similarities with that of northern Portugal: for example, the *Caldo o crema a la gallega*, containing sprouting turnip tops, is very like the famous Portuguese soup, *Caldo verde*; the *Caldeirada gallega*, a dish akin to *bouillabaisse*, is more or less identical with the dish of the same name from over the frontier; while the piquant *Callos a la gallega* (Galician-style tripe), a revelation to those accustomed only to the bland English version with onions, can only be compared with the famous *Tripas à modo do Porto*. On no account miss the *Empanada gallega*, a thick tart filled with onions, tomatoes and peppers, together with either sardines or loin of pork.

The shellfish from places like Cambados and Bayona is legion and of superb quality and freshness. It includes lobsters, langoustines, scampi, prawns of all shapes and sizes, spider crabs, scallops, clams and mussels. These may either be eaten cold with a mayonnaise, in *paella* or *Zarzuela*, or hot with imaginative sauces, as in the *Conchas de peregrino* (scallops), named after the famous pilgrimage to the shrine of St. James at Santiago de Compostela. The natural partner is the dry white *vino verde* from the region. If you want to experiment with the red *vino verde*, drink it stone cold, on a picnic or with one of the heartier Galician dishes such as tripe or *Empanada*.

PART TWO

PORTUGAL

7

The Land and History

As a broad generalisation Portugal falls into two geographical and cultural regions: the mountainous north and the wide plains of the Ribatejo and Alentejo south of the River Tagus, which flows into the Atlantic at Lisbon. The bulk of its best wine is made in the rugged north, where the ground rises progressively from a narrow coastal strip to the high sierras of the Spanish border. Whereas the south is predominantly dry and sunny, the north, like Galicia, is wet and humid apart from the summer months of June, July, August and September.

Although the population of Portugal is one-third that of Spain, her land area is only one-fifth; and as Professor Dan Stanislawski has so clearly set out in his scholarly *Landscapes of Bacchus* (University of Texas Press, 1970), this has had a profound influence on agriculture:

> Few places in the world support a more numerous rural population than does northwest Portugal. Anomalous in Portugal as a whole, this population is not concentrated in cities and towns but dispersed throughout the countryside on thousands of small properties cultivated with the devotion that is shown by gardeners.

The hunger for land has resulted both in the polyculture of the *vinho verde* area and in the terracing of the steep hillsides of the Douro Valley; these, in combination with the climate and soil, have given birth to the country's most individual wines.

In the area south of the Minho, marking the border with Galicia, the peasant festoons the vines on the trees at the edge of his plot or trains them high on granite posts, so releasing the rest of his land for food crops, such as the tall '*couve*' (Portuguese cabbage) or maize. While keeping the grapes well clear of the damp ground and affording a valuable break from the prevailing Atlantic winds, the disadvantages of this method are that grafts introduced after the calamitous *phylloxera* epidemic of the late nineteenth century are not as well suited to climbing as the native vines, and the spraying and harvesting of the fruit, necessitating long ladders, are laborious and at times dangerous tasks.

The soil is in general granitic, and if it has not been decomposed by the action of the weather, it must be broken up manually. Such back-breaking labour is even more typical of the port wine area in the Douro Valley just south, where the hard pre-Cambrian schist is not affected by prevailing conditions of climate. Not only must terraces be blasted in the hillsides and walls built to retain them, but the ground must further be broken up to receive the vines. With the rising price of labour, it has become a problem to maintain even the existing terraces.

Trellised vines in the Vinho Verde area

South again in the mountain-bound enclave of the River Dāo, the soil is granitic and of a varying degree of hardness, and some of it may be broken up fairly easily for planting. As in the port area there are great extremes of temperature. A maximum of 38°C/100°F has been recorded in summer, and temperatures of below freezing point during the other eight months of the year. Here, as in the Douro Valley and in other more southerly regions, the vines are grown low, but sometimes supported by stakes and wires.

Of other demarcated regions, Setúbal, Bucelas and Carcavelos, small and near Lisbon, and the larger and newly demarcated Bairrada south of Oporto are in coastal regions where limestone and clay predominate. Colares, with its sandy soils, which, alone in Europe, enabled the vines to withstand the ravages of *phylloxera*, deserves more detailed description later (see page 92).

The bulk of *consumo* wine (*vin ordinaire*) drunk in Lisbon and Oporto is supplied from undemarcated regions rather north of Lisbon and inland from the coast, where the vines are grown low in vast unbroken expanses; but in the southern part of the country very little wine at all is produced, except in isolated enclaves near Évora and in the now demarcated Algarve.

The reasons for the disappearance of once-flourishing vineyards from southern Portugal are historical. The early history of the country is that of the Iberian Peninsula as a whole, since it was not until the twelfth century that Afonso Henriques established a kingdom independent of Spain. It seems likely that viticulture was first developed by the Phoenicians and extended by colonists from Greece and Rome. Roman *dolia* have been discovered, closely resembling the *tinajas* still used in the south of Spain (see page 16) and in the Alentejo; and the geographer Strabo reported on the spread of viticulture along the western coast of Iberia during the first century B.C.

In Lusitania, the Roman province embracing southern Portugal, as elsewhere in the Peninsula, the all-conquering Moors did little to discourage the making or drinking of wine; and it was about the time of the Christian Reconquest that the vines disappeared, when the land was parcelled out among the new nobility and used either for hunting or growing wheat. The tradition of the large estate, and often absentee landowner, persists and has resulted in agrarian unrest in the region.

England has traded extensively with Portugal since the end of the thirteenth century, a partnership which resulted in the alliance of 1373, maintained ever since. As early as the twelfth century a wine named 'Osey', probably from the Oporto area, was popular in England and is mentioned in an early poem:

> Portyngalers...
> Whose merchandise cometh much into England
> Their land hath oil, wine, osey, wax and grain.

Osey continued to be shipped until relations between the two countries were broken off, when Philip II of Spain marched into the bereaved country in 1580 soon after the disastrous defeat and death of King Sebastian in Morocco, and successfully claimed the crown – to which he in fact had a title. Meanwhile, from the late thirteenth century, wine was also being exported from Monção on the northern border and was shipped from the neighbouring ports of Viano do Castelo and Caminha; and there are references in English literature to a mysterious wine called Charneco. In the play *Wit without Money*, written prior to 1600, there is a warning to avoid an inn 'where no old Charnico is nor Anchoves'; and in Shakespeare's *Henry IV*, Part II, the unfortunate Horner the Armourer drunk deep of Charneco before being killed in the duel with his terrified apprentice.

After the restoration of the Braganças in 1640 and strained relations with the Commonwealth, a new treaty with England was signed in 1654 and an attempt was made to popularise the

Douro wines, but, coarse and clumsily vinified, they were received with less than enthusiasm:

> Mark how it smells. Methinks, a real pain
> Is by its odour thrown upon my brain.
> I've tasted it – 'tis spiritless and flat,
> And it has as many different tastes,
> As can be found in compound pastes...

However, with England and France moving towards open war over the issue of the Spanish Succession, the famous Methuen Treaty was signed in 1703. Framed with the object of ending the trade in claret, it gave preference to Portuguese wines, and strenuous efforts were now made to improve them.

The Douro grapes were rich in sugar, and the problem was the rapid fermentation in conditions that led to the complete elimination of residual sweetness in the wine. A solution was found by adding brandy to the wine to arrest the last stages of fermentation, so leaving a little of the natural grape sugar. It required years of work on the part of the growers and the English shippers, who settled in Oporto in increasing numbers, before the process was perfected. At times desperate expedients were resorted to – such as the addition of elderberry juice to 'improve' the colour and flavour – and it was to eliminate mistakes of this sort and also the exploitation of the growers that in 1765, to the disgust of the English shippers, then banded together as the Association of Port Wine Shippers, the Marquês de Pombal instituted a government monopoly. Both Pombal's Port Wine Company and the Methuen Treaty itself were dissolved in the course of time, leaving the trade firmly in the hands of the British.

It was incidentally in Oporto that the first cylindrical bottles, which thereafter made possible the prolonged ageing of wines in glass, were first introduced about 1770. Previous to this the bottles in use, both in Portugal and elsewhere, were squat in shape and were necessarily stored upright. The use of corks as stoppers, common in the ancient world but later discontinued, had long since been rediscovered and put to good use by Dom Pérignon in making Champagne; but a cork out of contact with the liquid soon shrinks and becomes porous, and the air bubble below it is a breeding ground for harmful organisms that filter through. The new idea of binning bottles on their side to provide a liquid seal, in combination with corks of excellent quality made from the bark of the cork oaks so plentiful in Portugal and Spain, made possible first the creation of vintage port and later the splendid French vintage wines of the nineteenth century, after the new form of bottle had been introduced to Bordeaux from Portugal. For many years the traditional port bottle has had a slightly bulging neck to allow for expansion of the 'full long' (2 inch) cork, now used only for the vintage wines. A modified form of bottle with a straight neck is currently being introduced for Portuguese bottlings.

The island of Madeira was discovered in 1419 during the course of an expedition despatched by Prince Henry the Navigator. His captain, João Gonçalvez, or O Zarco ('the cross-eyed'), named it so because at the time it was covered with trees – and the Portuguese word for wood is *madeira*. Accidentally or not, its first colonists burned down the forests, so making way for the Malvasia (or Malmsey) vines introduced by Prince Henry.

Its wine was being exported as early as 1460; it is said to have been a favourite at the Court of Francis I of France and is mentioned anachronistically by Shakespeare in *Henry IV*, Part I:

> Jack! how agrees the devil and thee about thy soul
> that thou soldest him on Good Friday last for a cup
> of Madeira and a cold capon's leg?

In 1662 Madeira came under British control as part of the dowry of Catherine of Bragança on her marriage to Charles II, and during the next two decades English merchants established themselves in force and became the leading shippers. The trade received a great fillip in the early eighteenth century, when England's American colonists discovered a loophole in the edict that nothing from Europe might be shipped to the plantations or colonies except in English vessels. Madeira was, after all, far from the European mainland and off the coast of Africa; numerous further British firms moved in and engaged in direct shipment of the wines to the eastern seaboard of America. It is for this reason that Madeira is still much appreciated in the United States. It was also much drunk in the messes of the British army in Imperial India, where it was labelled 'SSS' ('Subalterns' soothing syrup'), it being supposed that young officers from home were unequal to port until fully acclimatised.

The island was briefly occupied by British troops in 1801, and they returned by mutual agreement in 1806, remaining until the end of the Peninsular War in 1814. Their quartermaster, John Blandy, stayed behind to found one of the great Madeira dynasties; his descendants still live on the island and control the firm of Blandy's Madeiras Lda. As a result of the interruption in supplies of wine from France, Portugal and Spain during the Napoleonic Wars, Madeira became the Englishman's wine *par excellence*. Exports had dropped steeply by 1825, even before the double scourges of *oidium* and *phylloxera* in 1852 and 1872, and the splendid fortified wines have never regained their former popularity in Britain, although there has been something of a comeback in recent years.

Port and Madeira were the shining exceptions to the low standard of other Portuguese wines; and when Gladstone repealed the Methuen Treaty in 1860, English consumption of the other wines fell dramatically. To quote from the Portuguese entry in the catalogue of the London International Exhibition of 1874:

> Damn was produced by careless and unskilfulness of productor... The drawing out from a great vessel of a little quantity of wine is always a great danger to wine extracted. To this process it must have very much attention and experience and cleanliness, when two thirds parts, at least, of Portuguese productors, which furnished samples, are entirely despisers of this matter.

It was to remedy this situation that in the early years of the present century the Portuguese Government began demarcating the wine-growing areas, laying down standards and setting up co-operatives where the peasants could take their grapes to be vinified by scientific methods. The result has been an immense improvement in the quality of table wines such as Dão.

Old-fashioned ox-cart used for transporting must to the adega

Without covering an excessive mileage, a fortnight's tour will give you a good preliminary insight into the different types of wine and the methods of production. You may start your trip by flying to Lisbon or Oporto, or enter the country by road either from Galicia or the Spanish Extremadura.

8

What the Wines Are

Portuguese wine lists often distinguish between *vinhos verdes* and *vinhos maduros*; and this is a natural outcome of the importance of the young and *pétillant* 'green wines' – most of them, in fact, red in colour – which account for about a quarter of the country's total production. Apart from port and Madeira, the *vinhos maduros* ('mature wines') include Dão and the demarcated wines of the centre (Bucelas, Carcavelos, Colares and Setúbal), together with a variety of undemarcated wines and the rosés, such as Mateus, which are exported abroad in such vast quantity.

Port

The making of port has not changed in essentials since Victorian times except in the method of crushing the grapes and in the employment of improved vats for fermentation. Some twenty varieties of grape are used for making the red wine, among the best-known, the Bastardo, Mourisco, Tinta Cão, Tinta Roriz, Touriga Nacional, Touriga Francesa and Tinta Francisca (descended from the French Pinot Noir).

Harvesting in the Upper Douro Valley takes place in September; the wine was traditionally made in open granite tanks or *lagares* with gangs of barefoot labourers treading the grapes, and most picturesque the routine was – and still is, where it survives. By 1960 labour had become so scarce that some of the Portuguese firms began experimenting with mechanical methods, and a number of the English houses, including Sandeman, Croft and Warre, followed their example. Modern practice is to use centrifugal crushers and then to ferment the must in lined concrete vats, designed like a coffee percolator to take advantage of the evolving gas to distribute the contents and break up the *manta* (or cap) of floating skins and pips. Some of the houses prefer to ferment in large open cement tanks with automatic pumping up of the must and its forcible spraying over the floating cap so as to break it up and submerge it, while others again, like Sandemans, ferment in stainless steel tanks; it is usually only the smaller farmers, unable to afford expensive new equipment, who still use the traditional stone *lagar*. The consensus of opinion is that the new procedures do not affect the quality of the wine.

As fermentation proceeds, with the conversion of grape sugar to alcohol, the amount of sugar in the must is measured with a saccharimeter. Once the concentration has fallen to between eight-and-a-half and six degrees Baumé, according to the requirements of the shipper, the must is run into large wooden casks, known as *toneis* and capable of holding some thirty pipes of wine, together with grape spirit of 77° strength to cut further fermentation. No smoking is allowed during this operation – the atmosphere of the *adega* is heady with the rising fumes of brandy – and once the contents have been thoroughly mixed with a 'lotting' pump, the *lote* of new wine is put aside to rest.

On average, well over 200,000 pipes of wine are produced annually, but only 80,000 are made into port; a points scheme, which takes into consideration the position of the vineyard, the form of cultivation and grape variety, and, very important, the yield from the grapes (a *low* yield is preferable), is in use to assess the suitability of the new wine for further elaboration. After resting at the *quinta* (estate or farm property) until the spring, it is transported to the port lodges of Vila Nova de Gaia, near the mouth of the Douro and opposite Oporto proper. The traditional sharp-prowed *barcos rabelos*, in one of which the famous port pioneer J.J. Forrester met his death in the rapids (see pages 111–12), later gave way to trains, but now most of the wine is unromantically brought down in tanker lorries to begin its years-long maturing, described in more detail later.

STYLES OF PORT

Of the different types of port, vintage port is made exclusively from grapes harvested in a particularly good year – on average, one in every five (see page 104). After two years in wood, the subsequent longer period of maturation takes place in bottle. It throws a heavy crust or sediment, which clings to the side of the bottle, and must be decanted. It is incidentally a popular fallacy that port will keep indefinitely, and vintage port that is more than thirty years old should not be bought without sampling it. Some vintage ports may be drunk when they are only ten years old, but they are often at their peak at fifteen to twenty. The interested reader should refer to George Robertson's *Port* or Ben Howkins' *Rich, Rare and Red* for complete lists of vintages firm by firm. One of the greatest of the century was that of 1931; Da Silva's Quinta do Noval is legendary.

Late bottled vintage port is kept for up to five years in wood, but consists entirely of wine of the same vintage and develops a ruby colour and a vintage flavour and bouquet. It has sometimes and unfairly come into disrepute for being sold in restaurants as vintage port, and also because blends of full-bodied ruby have been passed off in its name. It does not throw a crust and is therefore particularly suitable for people who like a good port, but have no cellar in which to keep it.

Crusted port differs from the vintage wine in being a blend of *lotes* (or parcels) of two or three different vintages; it is aged rather longer in wood, maturing more quickly, but also spends a prolonged period in bottle and throws a crust or deposit – hence the name. It is lighter-bodied, ready to drink in five to eight years and less expensive than vintage port, but without quite its individuality, and much resembles vintage character port, blended from first-class wines, not all of which were necessarily made in vintage years.

Tawny port is a blend of different vintages, which undergoes lengthy maturing in cask. The bottle is in effect simply a decanter, and the lighter-coloured, more delicate wine is a favourite with people who find the vintage and crusted ports too taxing. It has been much abused, since there are 'tawny ports' on the market, which owe their pale colour to the blending of cheaper light-coloured wines: indeed, the worst may even contain white port. The genuine article is by no means cheap, and fine old tawny is the wine which many of the shippers themselves most love and share.

Because of the relative infrequency of vintage years, the great bulk of port shipped abroad is wood port, defined as a blended wine matured in cask until it is ready for drinking. The best-known type is Ruby. Aged for only two to three years, it may greatly improve if kept in bottle for a few years more.

An old-fashioned Barco Rabelo *lying off the quays at Vila Nova de Gaia*

Apart from these ports made from black grapes, there are also white wines, always matured in wood and often made from Rei and Fina, varieties of Malvasia. These white ports were formerly sweet or very sweet, without the subtlety of the reds, but more recently the shippers have introduced dry white ports, made by fermenting out the grapes before brandying the wine, and are marketing them as apéritif wines.

In addition to these styles of port supplied by the British shippers, the Portuguese houses such as Ferreira and the Real Vinícola make others less familiar to British wine-drinkers. You may well enjoy their markedly different style and flavour and should make use of the opportunity to try them.

Portuguese barmen may incidentally tell you that port is not fortified. This is not true. Like sherry, it always undergoes fortification, which is indispensable to its very existence as a wine.

Madeira

The different styles of Madeira take their names from the grape varieties used in making them, although there has been some abuse of varietal names and some of the wines have been made only partially from the varietal name appearing on the label. All are fortified and matured in entirely characteristic fashion by the 'stoving' or heat treatment described later (see page 117).

Sercial, the driest, is fermented to completion so as to consume most of the sugar. It develops slowly and is not ready for drinking until at least seven years old. It is best drunk as an apéritif or with soup.

Verdelho is sweeter than Sercial with a full nutty flavour and becomes drier on the palate with age. It still goes well with soups or, for example, at teatime with a slice of the traditional Madeira cake.

Bual and Malmsey are made either by the addition of *vinho surdo*, a sweetening wine, or by adding sufficient spirit to arrest fermentation and so leave part of the grape sugar in the wine. Bual is golden-brown and fairly sweet, while Malmsey is very definitely a fragrant, rich and luscious dessert wine.

Vinhos Verdes

The *vinhos verdes* (pronounced 'veenyos verdsh') or 'green wines' are Portugal's most individual wines apart from port and Madeira, and only the neighbouring region of Galicia in Spain makes anything similar. They are so called, not because the wine is green in colour – they are in fact produced in the proportion of 70 per cent of red to 30 per cent of white, which is better-known abroad – but because of their youth and freshness. The fruit from the high-growing vines is picked in the early autumn and contains relatively less sugar and more malic acid than that from the normal low-growing vines. Normal methods of vinification would result in harsh, over-acid wines; but thanks to a secondary fermentation brought about by naturally occurring bacteria, the bulk of the acid is broken down with the evolution of carbon dioxide gas. It is by retaining it that the *vinhos verdes* emerge with a slight impermanent sparkle or *pétillance*, which varies from a mere prickling on the tongue with the maturer white Alvarinhos to a pressure of a few atmospheres in the case of some of the red wines.

Until special methods were devised for producing a longer-lasting and more pronounced sparkle, champagne was made by just this method and even drunk from the barrel, as are the *vinhos verdes* in country districts.

At their best, the white *vinhos verdes*, which in fact are pale lemon in colour, are low in alcohol, dry and somewhat astringent, but not unduly acid, and possess a flowery bouquet and delicate taste of fruit, more marked, in my opinion, than in a wine that is fully sparkling. They make most refreshing drinking in hot weather and, like the reds, should of course be chilled. In Raymond Postgate's memorable phrase, the red wine 'is unrelentingly hard, and the first mouthful is a shock'. He nevertheless adds that 'Red *vinho verde* is an experience worth having – on a sunny day, on the grass, with garlicked food and in the company of people who like wine from the cask, for that is what it will remind them of.' It is an acquired taste, but worth persisting in, if not at a picnic, with the stronger dishes from the region.

The demarcated area stretches from the Galician border and the River Minho in the north to somewhat south of Oporto and the River Douro. It is bordered by the Atlantic in the west and the port-growing region of the Upper Douro to the east. There are four types of black grape widely used in the region as a whole: Azal, Borraçal, Padeiro and Vinhão. The Azal branco, Esganoso, Loureiro, Pedernã, Rabigate and Trajadura are the most widespread of the white grapes.

As long ago as 1908 six sub-regions were recognised, differing in microclimate and the quality of their wines; in a general southward direction, these are Monção, Lima, Braga, Penafiel, Basto and Amarante. You may find it difficult to tell from which of these a particular proprietary wine comes, since much of it is made in a co-operative in the first place and sold in bulk for bottling and labelling by private firms, often in their wineries at Oporto.

Monção by general agreement makes the best white wine of the whole demarcated region, from the Alvarinho and Loureiro grapes. Alvarinho grapes are nevertheless scarce and account for only 2 per cent of the production of the sub-region; because of the higher alcohol content and lower than average effervescence, the Portuguese regard the wines made from them as half way towards a *vinho maduro* (matured table wine). Like the Albariño from Fefiñanes, they are sometimes compared with Moselle in respect of their lightness, elegance, recognisable acidity and flowery bouquet. The best of the wines from the Basto, centring on the valley of the River Tamêga, are from Celorico de Basto 900 ft up; they are rather less *pétillant* than average and contain some 9° of alcohol. Amarante, lower in altitude than the Basto and bordering the Douro River, makes rather heavier and stronger wines; and the reds are noted for their deep colour.

There is general agreement in Portugal that the best wines come from Monção, the Basto and Amarante; those from Braga, the largest producer of *vinhos verdes*, are nevertheless pleasantly sharp and effervescent. Penafiel, next in terms of production, makes wines resembling those of Amarante, if not quite matching them in quality. The other sub-region, lying along the valley of the River Lima, is in the main a producer of red wines. Heavier and lacking the verve of the others, they appeal to people who like something stronger and fuller-bodied, more similar in style to a *vinho maduro*.

Dão

The Dão, which supplies a large proportion of the best *vinho maduro*, both red and white, is an upland region in central Portugal, cut off from the rest of the country by high mountain chains and watered by a network of rivers flowing into the Mondego. It centres on the historic old town of Viseu, the meeting place of at least six Roman roads, and takes its name from the lesser River Dão, whose course lies entirely within the region.

The region grows a profusion of different grapes; and the Federação dos Vinicultores do Dão, the present controlling body, has encountered difficulties in persuading the smallholders to pull up inferior types and to replant with approved varieties. These are: for the red wines, Touriga Nacional, Alfrocheiro Preto, Tinta Amarela, Tinta Pinheira, Alvarelhão and Jaen; and for the white, Arinto do Dão, Borrado das Moscas, Cerceal, Barcelo, Encruzado and Verdelho. Only in the outlying areas are the vines terraced or grown high; elsewhere they are planted singly or in continuous trailing cordons, supported by stakes and wires and not exceeding 2 ft in height.

As late as 1949, Virgilio Correira de Loureiro, in a study commissioned by the Federação, could write of pressing and first fermentation being carried out in granite tanks. The wine was then run into barrels, where fermentation continued more slowly in the cool of a cellar and was further delayed by the onset of cold weather, resulting in the formation of glycerine, which gave the wines the smoothness for which they are still noted.

The picture has since changed completely. Although the grapes are still grown by smallholders, the larger proportion of the wine is made in ten modern co-operatives sited in the main areas of production. When the red Dão has been aged in wood for several years, it emerges dry, strong, deep in colour and full-bodied, more after the style of Burgundy than claret. Somewhat 'earthy' in flavour, the wines are often described as 'velvety' – an attribute resulting from their glycerine content. The white wines, much less numerous than the reds, develop their bouquet and flavour early, and the best are dry, clean and 'flinty'.

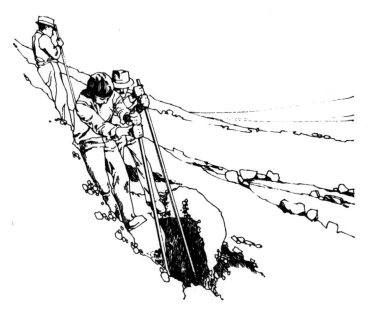

Breaking up the ground prior to the planting of vines in the Dão

The demarcated area is divided into three sub-regions, differing in microclimate and exposure. The two best are to the north-west and south-east of the River Mondego; but it is very difficult to obtain a single growth or, in fact, to establish the local origin of a typical Dão wine. This is because the co-operatives do not themselves keep the wine beyond the spring or summer after the harvest, but sell it to private firms, who transport it by tanker to their *adegas* (wineries), often outside the area, for maturing in wood and blending. In effect, the rapid transition from the peasant *adega* to the modern co-operative has resulted in an immense overall improvement in quality, and some of the red *reservas* matured by private firms are round and satisfying; but one is left with the feeling that the Dão has yet to produce the individual growths of which it is capable.

Demarcated Wines of the Centre

All four of these regions – Bucelas, Carcavelos, Colares and Setúbal – are of great historical interest and produce wine of high quality, but in very limited quantity. Two of them, Carcavelos and Colares, on the Atlantic coast near Lisbon, face eventual extinction because of the progressive encroachment of urban commuters and the profitable selling of plots for holiday villas.

In minuscule amount, Bucelas and Carcavelos produce white wines of great distinction, both favourites with Wellington's officers during the Peninsular War. They are described in a later section (page 102).

Colares has traditionally made some of the best and most individual red wine in Portugal. What makes the area unique is that the vines grow in sand dunes. Before they can be planted, a trench must be dug down to the level of the Mesozoic clay some 10 to 30 ft below, and the root is then sunk in a hole made with an iron bar. The man at the bottom works with a basket over his head, so as to avoid suffocation if, as sometimes happens, the sides of the trench suddenly collapse; and to avoid inordinate labour the young vines are encouraged to grow lateral shoots with subsidiary roots, so that the mother vine may 'creep' for up to 30 ft, giving rise to what are apparently individual plants. During the *phylloxera* scourge of the 1870s and 1880s, the insect could not penetrate the deep bed of sand, and the Ramisco vines have survived in their native form. The wine, astringent and rich in tannin, was likened by P. Morton Shand to 'one of the fuller Beaujolais, such as Juliénas'.

Setúbal, in the Arrábida peninsular just south of Lisbon, grows some good red table wine and manufactures large amounts of a carbonated rosé for export, but is demarcated only in respect of the Moscatel de Setúbal. It is made from a blend of grapes, both white and black, from various varieties of Moscatel vines, and fermentation is arrested by the addition of alcohol so as to leave some of the grape sugar. Its intensely fresh and fruity flavour is achieved by steeping grape skins in the young wine, which is then rested in wood until its first racking in the spring after the harvest. Moscatel de Setúbal, some of which is matured in oak for fifty years or more, must rank among the best dessert wines in the world.

Bairrada

The Bairrada, situated in the coastal province of Beira Litoral lying between Oporto and Coimbra, has as long a history of wine-making as any of the major regions in Portugal. Its demarcation has been a heated issue for decades, but was finally achieved only in 1979.

The region is known for two very different types of wine: full-bodied reds, rich both in alcohol and tannin and benefiting by long maturation in cask; and sparkling wines made by the Champagne process. It might be said that the Bairrada is to Portugal what the Penedès is to Spain.

Some 90 per cent of the red wine is made from the black Baga grape and 80 per cent of the white from the Maria Gomes; but there are other characterful varieties such as the white Bical and also small plantations of foreign varieties, such as the Pinot Noir, Pinot Blanc, Gamay and Chardonnay, introduced from France when the manufacture of sparkling wine began towards the end of the last century.

At the extreme east of the region, across the main Lisbon-Oporto road, is the forest of Buçaco and the Palace Hotel, which in small quantity makes some of the best of all Portuguese table wines, particularly the reds available at the hotel in vintages dating back to 1927.

Undemarcated Wines

Wines are Portugal's largest single source of foreign currency; and the largest export, rather ahead of port, is of carbonated rosés, of which the best-known are Mateus and Lancers. They are made by allowing the skins of the grapes to remain in contact with the must during the first stages of fermentation, which is terminated early so as to leave a certain amount of sugar in the wine. The sparkle is not natural, but is achieved by refrigerating the wine and passing carbon dioxide into it under pressure. The Bastardo, Alvarelhão, Mourisco and Touriga grapes used for Mateus are grown in the Upper Douro Valley, but other manufacturers use fruit from varied sources; the wine is collected by tanker, stored in huge concrete 'balloons' (see page 106) and elaborated at a central winery.

The Upper Douro, demarcated only for the grapes used in making port, also produces some very drinkable red *tintos* and *claretes*, and one really outstanding red table wine, the 'Barca Velha' made in very limited quantity by the port house of Ferreira and obtainable only at the best restaurants in Portugal.

A prime purveyor of everyday wines to Lisbon is Torres Vedras, where Wellington set up elaborate defensive positions in the winter of 1809–10 during the Peninsular War and sub-sequently beat back Marshal Masséna's offensive on Lisbon. The region makes full-bodied red wines rich in tannin and also, in the small sub-district of Óbidos, the excellent red 'Gaeiras'.

Further east, the alluvial flats of the Tagus, the so-called Ribatejo, produce vast quantities of *consumo* wine like the sturdy red Cartaxo. Its best-known firm, Carvalho, Ribeiro and Ferreira, markets some fine old Ribatejo *garrafeiras* (old vintage wines) and also the deservedly popular 'Serradayres', lighter and more claret-like in style than Dão.

The far south produces no wine except in the small enclaves of Vidigueira, Reguengos de Monsaraz, Redondo and Borba, whose strong, deeply-coloured and fruity co-operative-made red wines are of more than local repute. A strip along the holiday coast of the Algarve has recently been demarcated. The Algarve wines are drinkable enough with a simple meal, but undistinguished; the white wine is preferable to the red, which is full-bodied, 'earthy' and high in alcohol.

9

Control and Labelling

It was the Marquês de Pombal who, in setting up his Oporto Wine Company in 1756 to control abuses in the elaboration of port and to curb the power of the British shippers, first demarcated a wine-growing area in Portugal. The 'Old Wine Company' has long since disappeared and in 1933 the Government instituted the present system of control, embracing three organisations: the Casa do Douro, supervising viticulture in the field; the Port Wine Shippers Association; and the Instituto do Vinho do Porto, charged with the overall supervision of the production and trading of port.

Because of the overwhelming importance of port, it was not until the early 1900s that official efforts were made to improve the quality of the other wines and seven districts were demarcated. These were: Bucelas, Carcavelos, Colares, Moscatel de Setúbal, Vinhos Verdes, Dão and Madeira. In the first place these regions were autonomously controlled, but in 1937 the Junta Nacional do Vinho (JNV), with headquarters in Lisbon, was set up to co-ordinate the activities of the different regulatory bodies, other than the Instituto do Vinho do Oporto, and has now superseded all of the local bodies apart from the Comissão de Viticultura da Região dos Vinhos Verdes and the Federação dos Vinicultores do Dão.

It has long been recognised that the system of demarcation, unchanged since the 1900s, was in urgent need of overhaul. Two further regions, the Bairrada and Algarve, have recently been demarcated, while the Decree Law of 7 June, 1979 has established a new category of 'determinate areas' as a step towards full demarcation. These are regions (listed in Appendix 4) well known for individual wines of good quality; and for the purposes of shipment to the Common Market countries the EEC Commission, in its legalistic jargon, recognises them as 'Quality Wines PSR' and permits them to be labelled as such.

The JNV exercises a wide degree of control and provides numerous services to the wine producers in the demarcated regions, the determinate areas and the country generally, paralleled by the activities of the Comissão in the Vinho Verde area and the Federação in the Dão. It keeps a register of producers and vineyards, authorises grape varieties and methods of viticulture and vinification, offers technical assistance, underwrites loans for the construction of new co-operatives and conducts laboratory tests and tastings. As far as the consumer is concerned, one of the most important functions of the organisations is to issue guarantees of the authenticity of wines meeting their specifications in the form of a *selo de origem*. This takes the form of a printed and numbered paper slip, varying according to the region, stretched across the cork and stuck to the neck of the bottle before capsuling.

The JNV also organises an annual *Concurso Nacional de Vinhos Engarrafados,* a nationwide competition embracing all the categories of bottled wine – with the exception of port and Madeira, but including apéritif wines, brandies (*aguardentes*) and marc (*bagaceira*). This, though tending to be overgenerous, is a most valuable assessment of the wines in all their variety, the prize winners receiving *Medalhas de Ouro* (gold medals), *Medalhas de Prata* (silver medals) and *Menções Honrosas* (honourable mention), and has proved a stimulus to the producers.

The Portuguese Wine List

When inspecting a Portuguese wine list the first thing is to decide whether you wish to drink a *vinho verde* or a *vinho maduro* (a 'mature wine' such as Dão). Some of the other terms commonly appearing on wine labels are:

Adega. As in the Spanish *bodega*, a concern which may have made, shipped or sold the wine.

Aguardente. Brandy

Bagaceira/Aguardente de Bagaceira. A potent spirit distilled like *marc* from grape skins and pips.

Branco. White

Bruto. Extra-dry (used only of sparkling wine)

Cava, Caves. *Literally* a cellar, but used of establishments making sparkling wines.

Clarete. Light red

Colheita/Colh. Vintage, e.g. Colh 1972

Doce/Suave. Sweet

Engarrafado. Bottled

Espumante. Sparkling

Garrafeira. A vintage wine with long bottle age, e.g. Garrafeira 1970.

Generoso. A fragrant apéritif wine

Licoroso. Fortified

Reserva. Mature wine of good quality

Região Demarcada. Demarcated region

Rosado. Rosé (often carbonated)
Seco, Meio seco. Dry, medium dry
Tinto. Full-bodied red
Velho. Old
Vinho de mesa. Table wine

10

The Regions

Organising a Tour

It is a much easier business to organise a tour of the Portuguese wine-growing areas than those of Spain, for the simple reason that the area to be covered is very much smaller. Most of the general recommendations still apply; though the countries, so alike in many respects, are different in others – perhaps as a result of a lingering historical rivalry. One practical point is that the evening meal is served earlier than in Spain, usually from 8 p.m. A car is a great convenience, if not a necessity, since the vineyards and wineries are often inaccessible. You may either fly to Lisbon or Oporto and hire, or drive overland through Spain. Some knowledge of Portuguese or Spanish is needed for visits to *adegas* (or wineries) in the country districts; most Portuguese understand Spanish, the difficulty is to grasp what they say in reply! In the hotels and large places generally, French is more useful than English. The Port lodges are usually able to receive visitors; elsewhere an introduction will smooth matters, and the manager or porter at a local hotel can sometimes help. For details of organised tours to Oporto, which include visits to the lodges and *quintas* and tastings, apply to a travel agent or the Portuguese National Tourist Office, 1-5 New Bond Street, London W1Y 9PE.

Hotel accommodation in Portugal is officially classified under the heads of hotels, *pousadas, estalagens* and *pensões.* The government-owned *pousadas,* often installed in historic buildings like the Spanish Paradors, are well-run and comfortable, but often so small that reservations must be made well in advance. In the country districts the *estalagens* or privately owned inns, signposted by the road, are reliable and moderate in price, while many of the pensions are by no means to be despised – it is in them that you will often find the most typical regional cooking. *Hoteis Portugal,* a handbook listing all the establishments, with details of facilities and prices and available free from the Portuguese National Tourist Office, is an indispensable guide. You will also find the local offices of the organisation in Portugal most helpful in telephoning ahead to make reservations.

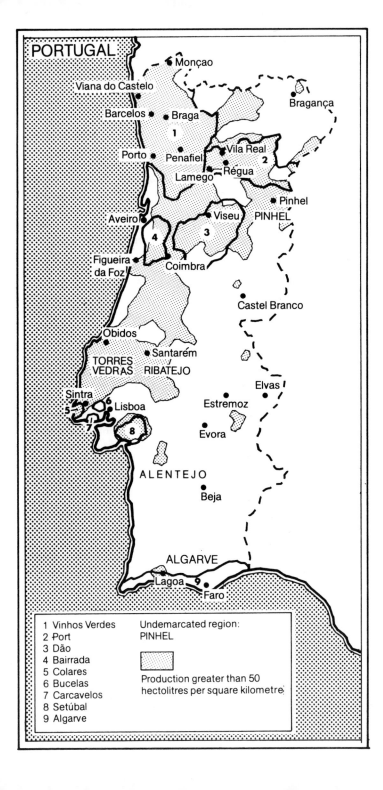

PORTUGAL

Monçao
Viana do Castelo
Barcelos · Braga
Bragança
1
Porto · Penafiel
Vila Real
Lamego · Régua
2
Pinhel
Aveiro · Viseu
PINHEL
4
3
Figueira
da Foz
Coimbra
Castel Branco
Obidos
Santarém
TORRES
VEDRAS
RIBATEJO
Elvas
Sintra
Estremoz
5
6
Lisboa
7
8
Evora
ALENTEJO
Beja
ALGARVE
Lagoa 9
Faro

1 Vinhos Verdes
2 Port
3 Dão
4 Bairrada
5 Colares
6 Bucelas
7 Carcavelos
8 Setúbal
9 Algarve

Undemarcated region:
PINHEL

Production greater than 50
hectolitres per square kilometre

Suggested Itinerary

If you arrive at Lisbon, the following overall itinerary may
serve as a basis for the trip. Spend a few days in Lisbon and its
environs, then head north for Oporto, either by the main N.1
through the old university town of Coimbra, or along the coast
if you want to take time out at its pleasant seaside resorts.
Explore Oporto and continue north into the *vinho verde* area,
making your centre at Braga, or Viana do Castelo on the coast.
From Braga, take the N.101 and the spectacular N.15 over the
heights of the Serra do Marão to Vila Real, a convenient base
for visits to Mateus and the port-growing area. Continue south
by the N.2 to Regua, the starting point for a side trip to see the
port vineyards and *quintas*, and then to the beautiful old town of
Lamego, which makes some of the best Portuguese sparkling
wine, and to Viseu. Stay for a day or two to explore the Dão
region, then proceed by the N.234 to Buçaco, well-placed for
visits to Anadia and Sangalhos, the main wine centres of the
Bairrada. Rejoin the N.1 north of Coimbra and return to
Lisbon.

This is simply a basic suggestion for covering the main wine-
growing areas without retracing your steps; and detailed routes
follow for the different regions. These regions are not, as in
Bordeaux or the Rioja, limited to the production of a single
wine (albeit red or white) of fairly well-defined type. For
example, Oporto on the fringe of the *vinho verde* area, is better
known for its Port lodges and is also the home of the huge
SOGRAPE plant making enormous amounts of carbonated rosé;
while the demarcated Port region, 80 km to the east, also
produces Mateus rosé, large amounts of red table wines and a
sparkling wine. Be prepared, therefore, for abrupt changes of
pace.

Wines of the Centre

The four demarcated areas are all within an hour's drive of
Lisbon, but rather than trek in and out of the city, you may
prefer to make your centre at Sintra, with its wooded crags and
palaces, 28 km to the west by the N.249. Its Palácio Dos Seteais
Hotel is probably the best and most elegant in the country. Do
not leave Lisbon without visiting one of its *fado* restuarants and
also the old Moorish quarter of the Alfama, where some of the
best regional cooking is to be had in its tiny and inexpensive
eating houses, or making the trip to Setúbal to the south.

Cross the Tagus by the great suspension bridge and follow
the motorway for Setúbal, leaving it for Vila Nogueira de
Azeitao. It is here that the best wines of the region are made by
the old-established firm of J. M. Da Fonseca. Its picturesque
'Old Winery' in Vila Nogueira, on a side turning doubling

back to the right of the main N.10, produces good red wines, and also the famous Moscatel de Setúbal.

The well-known 'Periquita' is made from a grape which took its name from the small farm, 'La Periquita' (Portuguese for a 'small parrot'), where José Mariá da Fonseca founded the firm in 1834. It is a fruity and full-bodied red wine aged in oak, always pleasant drinking, keeping well once the bottle has been opened and as good on the second day as the first. 'Camarate', formerly labelled 'Palmela', is a lighter wine containing a proportion of locally grown Cabernet Sauvignon, evident both in the attractive fruity nose and claret-like flavour.

The Moscatel is unique. Go and see the tiered oak casks in which it is matured until amalgamation with the brandy is complete, and, if you are fortunate enough to be invited, taste some of the older wines, of whose 'singular freshness of taste' H. Warner Allen wrote that it was as if the grapes had just been picked from the vine. The two generally available varieties are the six-year-old Moscatel de Setúbal and the twenty-five-year-old Moscatel Superior. There is also a red Moscatel Roxo not often found outside Portugal.

A few hundred yards further down the main road to the left is a very different establishment, resembling some futuristic moon-base with its gleaming white concrete 'balloons' for the bulk storage of wine destined for Fonseca's popular 'Faisca' and 'Lancers'. This new plant, planned and operated in conjunction with Hueblein Inc. of the USA, incorporates the latest innovations in hygiene and chemical engineering, and much of its large output is exported to America. Like Mateus, the wines appeal to that widespread public with a taste for a sweetish carbonated rosé.

Almost opposite the 'New Winery' on the opposite side of the road is a steep, tree-lined lane leading to the Quinta das Torres, one of Portugal's most atmospheric *estalagens,* installed in an old palace. In the dining room, embellished with splendid Italian majolica panels and overlooking a pool overhung by great trees, you may sample the local wines to the accompaniment of sophisticated and well-prepared food. Should you decide to stay at the Quinta or at the less isolated Pousada of Palmela, a reconstructed hill-top castle, explore the Serra de Arrábida behind, visit the charming coastal resorts of Sesimbra and Portinho and do not miss the Moorish gardens and palace of the Quinta de Bacalhoa a few kilometres further down the main road to Setúbal.

Carcavelos lies midway between Lisbon and Estoril on the N.6 to Sintra and is immediately accessible from either place – too much so for the survival of its once extensive vineyards, which long ago belonged to the famous Marquês de Pombal. Writing in 1929, P. Morton Shand described

Carcavelos as 'a dryish-tasting fortified wine, topaz-coloured, with a peculiar almond flavour that is usually not appreciated at the first glass'. Averaging 19° of alcohol, the wines vary from medium-dry to sweet and may be drunk chilled as a most individual apéritif or with a dessert. They are made in minuscule amount by a single remaining producer, Raul Ferreira & Filho, Lda.

The vineyards of Bucelas, although in no danger of disappearing, amount to only 450 acres centring on the valley of the Trançao River. They lie some 25 km north of Lisbon and 8 km to the west of the main N.1 or may be approached by a gentler cross country route from Sintra through Loures (see the large-scale Firestone Sheet 7). The Arinto grape, sometimes supposed to be a Riesling, makes light, dry, slightly acid wine with a delicate flowery bouquet; it is wine of this type which is exported, but in Portugal itself there is a taste for wines aged much longer in oak with a dry finish and hint of bitter almonds. There is only one producer, the firm of Camilo Alves, which labels most of its wines under the label of Caves Velhas.

Colares is only a few minutes' drive from Sintra along the N.247 towards the coast – the charming old tramway, which not so long ago took holiday-makers to the beaches, alas, no longer functions. When you arrive, take a good look at its entirely distinctive vineyards and, if visiting the area during winter or early spring, watch the planting of the vines through the sands. Another extraordinary feature is the palisades, woven of cane and willow and erected parallel to the coast, so as to protect the vines from the strong Atlantic winds and the salty spray from the sea. The area suffered a decline during the late nineteenth century, when the wines were brandied in imitation of port. Control now rests with the Junta Nacional do Vinho and the local co-operative, the Adega Regional de Colares, which vinifies all the wine on behalf of individual growers and bottles some of it under its own label. Red Colares – the whites are not of the same class – is aged in wood for an obligatory two years. Because of the high tannin content it is hard and astringent when young and must be aged in cask for as long as twenty years to emerge at its glorious best. Apart from the wines made by the Adega Cooperativa and the Real Vinícola do Norte de Portugal, some of the very best, labelled as 'Colares Chita' and 'Casal de Azenha' are from the cliff-top *adega* of Antonio Bernardino Paulo da Silva.

If you are leaving Sintra for Oporto and the north, an interesting route is by the N.9 and N.8 (but refer to a map) through Torres Vedras and Óbidos and on through Caldas da Rainha until you eventually join the main N.1. This will take you through Wellington's lines (see page 93) and the vineyards which now supply so much *vinho comun* (*vin ordinaire*) to Lisbon.

The old walled town of Óbidos, with its narrow streets and balconies overflowing with flowers, is one of the prettiest in the country. The castle at the top now houses a *pousada*; but its accommodation is so limited that you are much more likely to find a room at the Estalagem do Convento – no hardship, since it backs on to a charming garden and serves the excellent local 'Gaeiras', a dry red wine, fresh and fruity.

Oporto

There is a Portuguese proverb: 'Lisbon plays, Coimbra studies, Braga prays, Oporto works'; and Oporto, or in Portuguese Porto, the 'port', is the country's second city. It is in character that many of its best-known sights, like the suspension bridges across the gorge of the Douro, the arabesque stock exchange built in the nineteenth century, the eighteenth-century Factory House and the Port lodges are commercial in inspiration.

The Port lodges cluster along the southern bank of the Douro in Vila Nova de Gaia, opposite the city proper, which is built on steeply rising ground to the north. Old-fashioned buildings with red tiled roofs supported by wooden beams; many of them date from the eighteenth and early nineteenth centuries and were sited there to mature the wine brought down by river from the vineyards up country to the east. A few of the *barcos rabelos* used for this purpose, with their single high sails emblazoned with the names of their owners, may still be seen moored opposite the quay; and it was formerly a regulation that any wine exported as port had to be shipped over the sand bar at the mouth of the river.

The oldest of the port firms is said to be that of C. N. Kopke & Co. Ltd., founded in 1638 by Christian Kopke, the first consul-general for the Hanseatic Free Towns. English merchants, who in the first place had dealt in dried cod from Newfoundland (see page 120) and woollens in exchange for produce from Portuguese Brazil, moved into the wine trade when it became the custom to ship colonial goods direct from South America and an alternative commodity was sought. The senior English concern is Warre & Co., founded under another name in 1670; and Croft & Co. Ltd. began trading soon afterwards. Given the stimulus of the Methuen Treaty, others followed thick and fast during the eighteenth century and the early years of the nineteenth. The present trend is towards take-overs and mergers – Croft, for example, is now a subsidiary of International Distillers and Vintners Ltd. – but the firms scrupulously maintain the individual style of their wines, even when on occasion they call on their competitors for facilities unavailable in their own lodges, such as processing in modern refrigeration and filtration methods.

Although cement *cubas* (vats) are now used for the temporary storage of the wine, the lodges retain most of their traditional atmosphere. The young wine is first aged in large vats, often made of mahogany and containing as many as 180 pipes – the pipe is a 534-litre barrel used for the maturing and shipping of port. Further maturing of the wine is carried out in these wooden pipes, made of oak for the finer wines and chestnut for the others. They are fabricated on the premises, and it is fascinating to watch the coopers at work. After the planks have been cut and seasoned, they are fashioned into staves and softened in steam so that they can be bent into shape. The final stages are the hammering down of the metal hoops, the caulking of small gaps between the staves and the fitting of the flat wooden tops.

The pipes suffer a loss from evaporation of about 2 per cent annually – you will see fire warnings prominently displayed in the lodges – and when the wine is at intervals racked off the lees the casks are always filled up, sometimes with the addition of a little more alcohol to ensure that it remains healthy. The blending of the different *lotes* (or consignments from the vineyards) is a most intricate business and is controlled from the tasting room, where smoking is of course strictly forbidden. Records are kept of the characteristics and development of each and every *lote* from the time of its arrival.

Most port was formerly shipped in cask, and there was in the past a hallowed tradition that, because of climatic conditions, vintage port was best bottled in England, still its largest market. But it proved impossible to bottle the fine 1945 vintage in this manner, and the results of the Oporto bottling were so successful that all vintage port is nowadays bottled in the lodges. At the same time, more and more of the less expensive wine (amounting to about half of total exports) is being shipped in bulk in containers.

The declaration of a vintage year is a matter of great moment, taken only after careful examination of samples of the wine submitted to the Instituto do Vino do Porto and assessment of the likely demand for the wine. The different firms often concur in declaring a vintage, since conditions over the wine-growing area as a whole are generally much the same. One exception was the year of the outstanding Quinta Noval 1931, when only two shippers declared. Much earlier, in 1868, only Crofts failed to declare, a decision taken after an examination of the parched vineyards. Their director, J. R. Wright, left for Oporto on mule-back shortly after a fine rain set in and subsequently refused to change his decision. He nevertheless reaped a late benefit by selling the wine as '1869 Vintage' in a year when his rivals were unable to offer a vintage port.

Visits to the better-known lodges may be made without prior

arrangement, though it is advisable to check the hours of opening at your hotel. The guides speak English and the tour always ends with a tasting of the wines. Among the leading firms are:

Bermester	Martinez Gassiot
Butler Nephew	Morgan
Cálem	Niepoort
Cockburn Smithes	Offley Forrester
Croft	Quarles Harris
Delaforce	Quinta do Noval
Diez Hermanos	Rebello Valente (the vintage
Dow	mark for Robertson Brothers)
Ferreira	Robertson Brothers
Feuerheed	Sandeman
Fonseca	Smith Woodhouse
Gonzalez Byass	Taylor, Fladgate & Yeatman
Gould Campbell	Tuke, Holdsworth
Graham	Hunt, Roope
Kopke	van Zeller
Mackenzie	Warre

The British shippers form a close-knit community and have preserved their identity and traditions to a much greater extent than their former compatriots in Jerez. Their sons usually go to English schools and marry English girls. The most obvious symbol of this 'Britishness' is the Factory House in the Rua dos Inglezes ('Street of the English'), for centuries the commercial heart of the trade, near the quays in Oporto on the other side of the river from the lodges. You may easily enough inspect the uncompromisingly Georgian English façade of the building, constructed by the English merchants or 'factors' who in 1727 formed the Association of Port Wine Shippers, but to see the inside you need to be accompanied by a representative of one of the British shippers. It now serves as a club for the senior partners of the Association of the thirteen British port shippers, one of whom is elected Chairman (or 'Treasurer', as he is called) for a period of a year, during which he supplies all the wood ports to the club and also chooses the vintage port for the ritual Wednesday lunch of the members. The building houses a spacious entrance hall, a lofty granite staircase, a ballroom with ornate chandeliers and furniture in the manner of Chippendale, a fine cellar and a writing room, which, among other relics, houses copies of *The Times* from first publication and a visitors' book in which are inscribed the names of Wellington's officers, who were made honorary members after the recapture of Oporto from the French during the Peninsular War. An individual feature are the twin dining rooms, each laid for the same meal, and to the second of which the members and their guests adjourn for dessert so that they may taste their port well away from the aroma of cooking.

Apart from the Instituto do Vinho do Porto, the body responsible for maintaining the standards of port wine, Oporto is also the headquarters of the Comissão de Viticultura da Região dos Vinhos Verdes; and it is easy to lose sight of the fact that a great many of the firms which bottle and market 'green wine' operate from here. Another establishment, centuries away from the traditions of the port lodges, is the huge plant on the outskirts of the city, where SOGRAPE (Sociedade Comercial dos Vinhos de Mesa de Portugal) bottles the bulk of its Mateus Rosé (another huge vinification plant has more recently been opened at Anadia in the Bairrada). This winery, the largest in Portugal, is well worth a visit and there should be no difficulty if you telephone the head office in Oporto.

Concrete 'balloons' for storing wine at Azeitão

The history of Mateus is a dramatic one. In 1951 Sacheverell Sitwell 'discovered' the wine as far as England was concerned and wrote in the *Sunday Times* that it was 'the most delicious vin rosé that I have ever tasted'. Since then the energy of its proprietors, the Guedes family, has made it one of the biggest selling wines in the world – exports to the United States alone run to some 14 million bottles a year – the key to its success being that it is bought by people who do not normally drink wine with their meals and want something which they feel that they can safely drink with whatever they eat.

The wine has already been vinified when it arrives at the plant (see page 110) and, as at the Fonsecas' winery at Azeitão, is first stored in 'balloons', which are quickly and cheaply made by spraying concrete on to huge rubber balloons. After the concrete has set, they are deflated and removed, and the inside surface is sprayed with epoxy resin. The main buildings house cement or tiled vats in endless and serried rows, connected by miles of stainless steel piping; and the pumping, filtration and clarification procedures are often carried out without sign of human agency. It is here that the wine is blended, so as to achieve uniformity of flavour. The sparkle is not natural, but is carefully regulated by passing carbon dioxide gas under pressure into the refrigerated wine. D. Fernando van-Zeller Guedes, who numbers a sixteenth-century viceroy of Portuguese India among his ancestors, and his family are the most human and considerate of people and meticulous about the welfare of their employees. The winery incorporates a community centre, canteens, nursery school, surgery and sports facilities.

Vinhos Verdes

Without doing more than taking the N. 15 from Oporto to Vila Real and the port country, you can pass through the southern fringe of the *vinho verde* area and, by visiting the beautiful Aveleda estate of the Guedes family and the co-operatives at Penafiel or Amarante, form a good idea of the methods used in making the wines, whose characteristics and tastes have already been described (pages 88–90). Nevertheless, this hilly, well-wooded region, with its groves of chestnut, pine and sweet-smelling eucalyptus and its winding country roads banked with wild roses and hydrangea, is one of the most scenic in the country, and by going further north you will see all the varied methods of growing the vines, either strung from tree to tree, in dense 30 or 40 ft curtains by the roadside, in the form of roofed-in arbours supported by granite pillars or, in more modern vineyards, trained on wires strung between T-shaped uprights of wood or concrete, known as *cruzetas*. The enthusiast of 'green wines' should also certainly pay a visit to Monção in the extreme north to drink the Alvarinho on the spot at its delicious best.

If you make for the old cathedral city of Braga, 50 km along the N. 14 from Oporto, you will find yourself at the geographical centre of the region. A pleasant place to stay is at the Hotel do Elevador, so called because it is at the top of a funicular railway ascending to the famous Baroque shrine of Bom Jesus outside the city (the ascent may also be made by car or up the many hundred steps of the grand stairway). Whichever way you go from Braga you will be in the green wine country. An interesting round is to take the N. 103 to the charming old town of Barcelos, pausing to taste the local wine and continuing to Esposende on the coast, where the Quinta de S. Claudio makes one of the best of all *vinhos verdes*. Turn right and follow the N. 13 through Viana do Castelo and along the Minho estuary to the border post of Valença where there is a comfortable and atmospheric *pousada*. From there it is 18 km by the N. 101 to Monção, which faces Galicia across the river.

Lunch or stay the night at one of its *pensões* or small hotels where they may well help you in making visits to the local vineyards and *adegas*. Return to Braga through the pine woods of the N. 101 and from there through Guimaraes, the capital of the original County of Portucale, to the junction of the main Oporto–Vila Real road (if you have not yet visited Aveleda, take the N. 106 to Penafiel, otherwise continue along the N. 101, which joins the N. 15 short of Amarante). The climb towards Vila Real is one of the most spectacular in Portugal, with the road winding and returning on itself along the side of a great wooded gorge. The Pousada de São Gonçalo near the top of the pass, with its splendid panoramic views, is a delightful halting place if you wish to stop short of Vila Real (but book your room in advance).

HOW THE WINES ARE MADE

Before visiting one of the wineries it is as well to understand a little more about the process of vinification, involving the elimination of malic acid. All wines undergo a slow secondary fermentation, during which residual sugars are partially broken down and malic acid, which would otherwise give them a harsh taste, is largely eliminated. The amount of malic acid in the fruit from the *vinho verde* area is so high (up to 15 g/litre) that a modified and more extended secondary or malo-lactic fermentation is employed to reduce it. With other wines, malo-lactic fermentation in such marked degree is a defect, since it reduces the amounts of free acid to a level where the wines are exposed to pathogenic infection.

The first or tumultuous fermentation of the *vinhos verdes* is modified by carrying it out at relatively low temperatures and adding small amounts of sulphur dioxide to inhibit the growth of organisms inimical to the *Lactobacillus* and *Leuconostic* bacteria, which appear spontaneously in the lees (or residues) at the bottom of the vat and are responsible for the subsequent malo-lactic fermentation. Under their influence malic acid is converted into the smoother tasting lactic, with the formation of carbon dioxide, later liberated and retained in the bottle or barrel to give the wines their slight sparkle. The serious student can pursue this somewhat complex subject in *Le Vin Verde* by Amandio Barbedo Galhano, Oporto, 1951, and in the series of research papers published in the *Estudos, Notas e Relatórios* of the Comissão de Viticultura da Região dos Vinhos Verdes.

Red wines are fermented in contact with skins, pips and stalks; and the high tannin content contributes to their harsh flavour. The whites are made *bica aberta*; all the skins, pips and stalks are removed before fermentation.

The wines are not frequently racked, because this would

result in the disappearance of the *Lactobacillus* with the lees. They usually clarify without difficulty and are bottled in the February or March following the harvest. The *pétillance* develops a month or two later and when ready for drinking shortly afterwards the wines normally contain 8° to 11.5° of alcohol. Those from Monção are rather stronger.

It should be added that in the past, as still in small peasant *adegas*, secondary fermentation took place in barrels with the retention of all the carbon dioxide. Now that so much of the wine is made in the open cement vats of the co-operatives, much of the free gas bubbles away, so that it is often replaced by a little carbon dioxide from cylinders. More typical of a newer generation of *adegas* is that of the Palacio de Brejoeira on the outskirts of Monção, makers of a first-rate Alvarinho, pale, dry, fruity and elegant, which has been likened to a good Chenin blanc. Its installations include modern horizontal presses and stainless steel fermentation tanks.

Much of the wine is made in some twenty co-operatives, which either sell it under their own label or dispose of it in bulk to private firms for subsequent bottling. The system is much the same as in Spain. The farmers belonging to the co-operative contract to deliver their crop to a large central winery, constructed with a bank loan underwritten by the Junta Nacional. They are paid a certain amount in cash according to the weight and sugar content of their grapes and later share in the profits from the sale of the wine, provision being made for amortisation of the loan and running costs. The plants are managed by an executive committee of the growers, headed by a President, himself a grower and a man of local standing.

Whichever of the co-operatives you visit, you will find the same general arrangements. The cement vats for fermenting and maturing the wine stand at floor level in rows, with further underground storage capacity and facilities for refrigerating and bottling the wine. The plants are generally modern and of medium capacity: that of the Adega Regional de Monção, rather smaller than most, has a capacity of 600,000 litres – of this, only 20,000 bottles emerge as its excellent white Alvarinho. Unlike the typical co-operative in Spain, many of their Portuguese counterparts distil the skins and pips to make a very potent *bagaceira* or *marc*.

Apart from a co-operative, you should also try to visit one of the smaller private *adegas*. At that of the Vinhos de Monção Lda., all the wine is fermented in wood and matured in chestnut barrels. Total production, including a red wine and *bagaceira* as well as the famous white 'Cepa Velha', amounts to only 50,000 litres; there would be no point in extending the winery, since there is already keen competition for the very limited amount of Alvarinho grapes.

Either from Oporto or Braga, make a point of going to the Quinta da Aveleda, off the N. 15 near Penafiel. You will be most courteously received at this beautiful estate belonging to the Guedes family, who control SOGRAPE, the producers of Mateus Rosé and the excellent Dão 'Grão Vasco', as well as the 'green wines' from Aveleda. The grounds alone, with their groves of pine, oak and eucalyptus, the azaleas and hydrangeas, the trellised arbours and pools carpeted with water lily, are well worth the visit. The grapes are planted French style, with different varieties of vine on separate plots, which allows for more nicety in the making of the wine than is possible at a co-operative. The picturesque buildings house modern horizontal presses, cement-lined vats and a modern bottling line; at the same time some of the wine is matured in wooden casks. The guided tour ends with a most enjoyable tasting on a terrace overlooking the gardens and vineyards.

It is unusual to encounter the red *vinhos verdes* outside Portugal; the whites, light, delicate and refreshing with their elusive sparkle, make ideal summer drinking and have become increasingly available abroad. In Portugal itself the taste is for the traditional bone-dry wines, of which one of the most popular is the 'Casal Garcia' from Aveleda. Many of the wines are now available in the UK, though some, like 'Aveleda', have been slightly sweetened to the English taste, while the exceptionally fragrant and fruity 'Gatão' from Borges & Irmão is definitely sweet. Other representative wines with an authentic 'green' taste are 'Casaleiro', 'Casalinho', 'Magrico', 'Messias' and 'Verdegar' (the last from the co-operative union of Vercoope).

The Upper Douro

The best centre for the region is Vila Real, where the most comfortable place to stay is the Hotel Tocaio. Before setting out for the port vineyards, pay a visit to Mateus, 3 km east on the N. 322. The palace, in all its Baroque exuberance, figures on the elegant Mateus Rosé label and has no doubt done much to stimulate sales. If you wish, you may visit the grounds and the flamboyantly furnished interior. The Mateus winery and vineyards lie close by, and since the wine is actually vinified here (and not simply blended and elaborated as at the larger plant near Oporto) it is interesting to see it. The grapes, a proportion of which come from the surrounding vineyards, are black with a white pulp, the principal varieties being Bastardo, Alvarelhão, Mourisco and Touriga. The skins are allowed to stand in contact with the must for a short time to release colouring matter, and fermentation then proceeds as for a white wine. The residual sweetness is achieved by centrifugation or dosage with sulphur dioxide, so as to inactivate the yeasts before fermentation is complete, and to leave some of the grape sugar in the wine.

The winery also makes some pleasant Vila Real *tintos*; and, although not as yet demarcated except for port, the region as a whole is now a 'determinate area' (see page 95) and is making a lot of very sound red table wine. Other examples are the 'Evel' from the Real Companhia Vinícola do Norte de Portugal and those from Valpaços near Chaves, further to the east. Their manufacture has been made possible by the introduction of closed cement vats (*cubas de fermentação*), which allow a controlled fermentation, not possible in the days of the open stone tanks, when the fast and furious evolution of carbon dioxide carried away most of the bouquet and left the wine harsh and over-dry without residual sugar.

Of all the table wines from this area the best is the red 'Barca Velha' made by the port firm of Ferreira at their Quinta do Vale de Meão at the top of the Douro Valley only 40 km from the Spanish frontier. A favourite at the lunches held in the Factory House by the port shippers, it is a deep ruby orange with intensely fruity nose and flavour, round, full-bodied, complex and beautifully balanced. Vintages tend to be far between, and the only two available until the 1978 comes on to the market are the 1965 and 1966. Ferreira also makes a 'Ferreirinha Reserva Especial' with somewhat similar characteristics.

Ferreira is the largest of the Portuguese-owned port It dates from 1751, but owes its pre-eminence to a remarkable woman, Dona Antónia Adelaide Ferreira, born in 1810, who married her cousin, one of the richest men in Portugal at the time. It was he who founded the Quinta do Vesúvio, the largest estate in the Douro, and planted hundreds of thousands of vines in vineyards covering seven hills and thirty valleys. Dona Antónia remarried after his premature death and after the death of her second husband became the uncrowned queen of the Douro, ruling her vast estates with a severity matched only by her kindness and business ability. She died a multimillionairess. Her firm and characterful face, in blue and white tiles, looks down on the visitor today at the company's great lodge in Vila Nova de Gaia.

Dona Antónia was tragically linked with another of the great figures of the nineteenth-century port trade. Joseph James Forrester arrived from England in 1831 to join his uncle's firm, Webber, Forrester and Cramp (now Offley, Forrester) and soon made his influence felt. He was a talented amateur artist – the portraits of his contemporaries and his painting of the Rua Nova dos Inglezes are well known – and, as a result of his pioneer work in charting the Douro Valley and his services to the port industry, was created a Baron by the Portuguese

Government. He was a man of forceful opinions, and the publication in 1843 of *A Word or Two on Port Wine* , in which he attacked not only abuses such as the adulteration of the wine with elderberry juice, but also criticised its fortification with brandy, stirred up violent controversy. On 12 May, 1862, when returning down river to Oporto after a convivial lunch with the Baroness Fladgate and Dona Antónia at the Quinta de Vargellas, their boat capsized in the rapids; the two ladies, buoyed up by their crinolines, struggled ashore, but Forrester sank like a stone and his body was never recovered. The full facts of the accident are still obscure. It seems that the rudder was lashed the wrong way, and it is sometimes said that he was wearing a belt loaded with gold for paying his workers and that his death was contrived.

The most picturesque time to visit the port vineyards is during the harvest and the traditional treading of the grapes by night and by hurricane lamp, of whose climax Rupert Croft-Cooke wrote so evocatively: 'Now the band strikes up, now every man moves as he likes in the purple must, which covers his knees. Grinning, shouting, dancing alone or in couples face to face, twining their arms above their heads in curious serpentine movements, they never cease treading... They are as satyrs, they are crazy Bacchants, they have ceased to be quite human....'

By sober daylight and at other times of year, you can at least drive through this man-made landscape, where back-breaking toil has reduced whole mountainsides to regular terraces, with their neat stairways giving access from one level to another. One of the estates at Pinhão which you should try to visit is Croft's Quinta da Roeda, the so-called 'Diamond of the

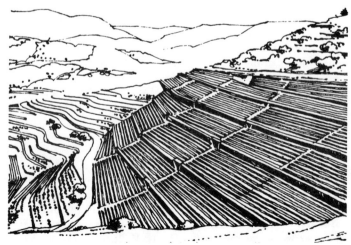

Terraced vineyards in the Douro Valley

Douro'. Sarah Bradford, in *The Englishman's Wine,* aptly writes of its residence and of the neighbouring property of Bomfim that 'Neither of them are in the architectural class of the French wine châteaux, nor were they intended to be. For a moment, looking at the steel-pillared verandahs, the shiny wooden floors, cream paint, cretonne and wicker chairs one could imagine oneself in a planter's house in the West Indies....'

Another estate of exceptional interest is A.J. da Silva's Quinta do Noval, which dominates the Pinhão Valley and produces some of the very best vintage port. The vineyards date from the eighteenth century, but its present superb terraces were planted later, in the nineteenth. Its present owners, the van Zeller family, have experimented with a new and wider form of sloping terrace, but also preserve a small area planted with the traditional ungrafted Nacional vines. Their upkeep, prone as they are to *phylloxera*, presents great difficulty, and although they produce a magnificent wine, the quantity is very small, amounting to only five to ten pipes a year.

To visit the port vineyards and *quintas*, continue from Vila Real along the N. 322 to Sabrosa and turn right down the N. 323 to Pinhão at the heart of the district and the railhead for wine despatched to Oporto by freight train, and if possible try to arrange in Oporto for a visit to one or more of the *quintas* belonging to the large port houses, where the wine is vinified and first matured. Apart from growing and vinifying their own grapes, the port firms also buy fruit from smallholders or wine from larger farmers – made under careful supervision. To see these little vineyards and wineries it is more or less essential to go with someone from one of the estates, as the precipitous mountain tracks are accessible only by Land Rover, and fluent Portuguese is a necessity.

The extreme south-west corner of the area demarcated for port produces a good sparkling wine. The *caves* may conveniently be visited en route from Vila Real to Viseu and the Dão. Take the N. 2 to the rail centre of Regua, cross the Douro and continue through the terraced vineyards to the historic old town of Lamego, where in 1142 the Côrtes (or parliament) recognised Afonso Henriques at the first King of Portugal. It is dominated by an eighteenth-century Baroque shrine, reminiscent of that at Bom Jesus and approached by a huge stairway springing dramatically from the tree-lined avenue at the centre. The extensive Caves da Raposeira, recently taken over by Seagrams and tunnelled deep into the rock, lie to the left of the road and about 1 km beyond. Short of an introduction, lunch at the Estalagem de Lamego, high in the woods above the town, and ask them to telephone. Apart from the best from the Bairrada, the sparkling wine made here by the Champagne method (see page 61), and sold under the name of

'Raposeira' is among the pleasantest produced in Portugal. As with the Spanish sparkling wine you should ask for the *bruto*, since *vinhos espumantes* labelled *seco* or *meio-seco* ('dry' and 'semi-dry'), and even more so the pink wines, are liable to be very sweet by British standards.

Dão

Continuing another 70 km southwards along the N. 2, you will come to Viseu. It is well worth spending some time here to visit the cathedral and the museum with its paintings by the renowned Grão Vasco and also to explore its narrow, hilly streets with old-fashioned shops that seem more Moorish than European. You may stay either at the luxurious Hotel Grão Vasco or at the elegant Estalagem Viriato in charming wooded surroundings outside the town. Viseu is the headquarters of the Federação dos Vinicultores do Dão and the winery where SOGRAPE makes its well-known Dão, named Grão Vasco after the painter; it is also a good centre for visiting the vineyards and wineries.

Although there are numerous different brands of Dão on sale, the companies which sell them have blended and matured the wine rather than made it. This is because the vineyards in the Dão are split up between a multitude of small farmers, and only the actual proprietor of a vineyard is permitted to vinify his grapes. There are only a few private firms like that of Casa Santos Lima in Silgueiros with a sizeable output (in their case of 500,000 litres annually), and only one estate-made wine, that of the Conde de Santar, is available on a commercial scale. More than half of the wine is made in the region's ten co-operatives; to get acquainted with the way in which it is made, the first thing is therefore to visit one or two of the co-operatives. You can do this by making a 54 km round from Viseu, which will take you through some typical wine-growing country, with the green vineyards dotted among darker belts of pine and expanses of naked granite.

Take the N.18 to Mangualde. Go into the village and first visit the Casa Anadia. With its huge umbrella-like plane tree in the courtyard, its landscaped gardens, its ornate reception rooms and blue and white tiles representing scenes from a fantasy world, it is one of the most beautiful smaller palaces in Portugal. You may have difficulty in obtaining admittance: pull resolutely on the bell in the wall and if necessary enlist the help of the villagers in finding the caretaker.

Just outside Mangualde to the right of the N.234 for Nelas is the large new co-operative, with a planned output of 4 million litres of wine annually. Its great cement *cubas de fermentação* are of the modern automatic type, providing for continuous submersion of pips and skins, and the new wine is rested through the winter in cool underground *depósitos*. The buyers from the wine companies arrive in January or February; and samples are drawn up through hatches in the floor in a long-handled cup, like the *venencia* (page 39). Both Mangualde and Nelas make some of the best Dão, large quantities of which are bought by SOGRAPE and the other big companies for blending and maturing. Continue along the N.234 to Nelas, stop if you wish to visit the smaller but very similar co-operative at Nelas, then turn right along the N.231 to Viseu. The country road will take you through vineyards with the typical cordoned vines and past a number of small private *adegas*.

If you want to see the vineyards in the more northerly part of the region, the best plan is to combine this with a visit to Buçaco on your return to Coimbra and Lisbon. The N.234 will take you through the heart of the district and past the co-operatives at Tondela and Santa Comba Dão. Another interesting visit, if it can be arranged through the hotel or local office of Turismo, is to the Quinta da Insua, some 40 km from Viseu, where a tiny winery attached to this most beautiful of mansions makes wines for private consumption from Sémillon and Cabernet grapes of French origin.

Having seen how the wine is grown and vinified, get in touch with the Vinícola do Vale do Dão at Viseu and ask if you may visit it – as at all the establishments controlled by the Guedes family, the staff is most attentive to visitors. The wine is first stored in the typical concrete 'balloons' and is then blended to achieve the desired style and matured in wooden casks for upwards of two years and for a further period in bottle. A tasting here of 'Grão Vasco' aged for different periods will give you as good an impression of the range and scope of Dão wine as you are likely to obtain. My own preference is to drink the whites young, whereas the reds gain greatly by prolonged maturing. In view of the way that they are made, it would be pedantic to draw fine distinctions between the wines sold under different labels; and this is borne out by the fact that some twenty-seven Dãos, red and white, gained gold medals at the last *Concurso*. Apart from 'Grão Vasco' and the estate-made wines from the Conde de Santar, others obtainable abroad include the excellent 'Terras Altas' from J.M. da Fonseca, the only large firm to maintain a winery in the district apart from SOGRAPE, and those from Caves de Primavera, Ribalonga, and the Bairrada firms of Aliança and Barrocão.

From Viseu go where you please – east through Guarda into Spain, south over the spectacular heights of the Serra da Estrela into the plain of the Alentejo to sample the sturdy red wines from Borba, Regengos de Monsaraz and Redondo east of the historic old town of Evora, or south-west by the N.234 to Coimbra and Lisbon. If heading for Coimbra do not fail to pay a visit to Buçaco, off the road to the left near its junctions with the N.1. This is the 'damned long hill' where Wellington gained his famous victory over Marshal Masséna in 1810; its forest is a nature reserve containing some four hundred varieties of trees and flowering shrubs. At the centre is the grandiose Palace Hotel do Buçaco, once a royal hunting lodge, where you may drink really remarkable vintage Buçaco wines from the extensive cellars originally laid down by the ill-fated King Carlos I, who was assassinated in 1908. From Buçaco it is well worth making a short detour to nearby Anadia and into the Bairrada before rejoining the main N.1 for Lisbon.

Bairrada

The Bairrada produces about as much wine as the Dão (some 480,000 hl of red and 22,000 of white in an average year), most of it a full-bodied red which repays long ageing because of the high content of tannin. Its wineries are known as *caves*, because all of them also produce large amounts of sparkling wines by the Champagne process – it is of good quality, but tends to be earthier and more definite than either Champagne or the Spanish sparklers from the Penedès.

Most of the *caves* are grouped in Anadia, the headquarters of a Government research station, the Estação Vitivinícola da Beira Litoral, or in Sangalhos, a few kilometres across the Lisbon-Oporto road to the west. Caves Aliança in Sangalhos ranks next to SOGRAPE and J.M. da Fonseca in terms of size, but its domestic sales are second only to those of SOGRAPE, and its reliable 'Tinto Velha Aliança', made mainly with Bairrada wine, is the biggest selling red wine in Portugal. Other Bairrada wines obtainable from specialist merchants in the UK are those from Caves Barrocão, Caves São João, Caves Império and Caves Messias. They include some excellent and very modestly priced red *reservas* and *garrafeiras*.

Madeira

Madeira is, of course, a great deal further afield than mainland Portugal, but wine-lovers holidaying in that delightful island may well wish to see something of the vineyards and the making of the wine.

The island is volcanic and mountainous and the vines are grown on terraces supported by large basalt blocks and are trained on trellises some 2 metres high. The best of the growths are from the south of the island and westwards of the capital, Funchal, from parishes such as Câma de Lobos, where Sir Winston Churchill was so fond of painting. Treading in a stone *lagar* is no longer practised except by small proprietors, and the shippers buy grapes rather than must, which are now pressed mechanically.

The 'stoving' of wines is a process peculiar to Madeira and is undertaken because it was found during the eighteenth century that wines transported in casks in the sailing vessels of the time improved with the shaking and heat of the tropics. In modern forms of *estufa* or stove the wine is heated for a minimum period of three months at 50°C or for longer at 45°C. Fortification of all but the very best wines takes place after stoving to avoid loss of alcohol. Even Current Madeira is not shipped until five years old, and the better wines are aged for longer periods, either in cask as vintage Madeira or in *solera* (see page 38).

Names of the leading shippers and of firms banded together as the Madeira Wine Association and sharing certain production facilities are listed in Appendix 2.

Spirits and Aromatic Wines

Brandy is produced on a large scale, many of the larger wine concerns operating a distillery in conjunction with their wineries, and is known as *aguardente* (although some of it is labelled 'brandy' or *brande*). The less expensive brandies are made as in Spain from a grape spirit distilled in a continuous column and subsequently diluted with water to about 44° (percentage by volume of alcohol) and matured in oak casks. The spirit is supplied to private firms by the government-controlled Administración Geral de Alcool, much of it being made from surplus red *vinho verde*. The better brandies are made in a simple copper still either by the Charentais method (see page 70) or by a single distillation in the manner of Armagnac. The darker and older brandies, labelled *reserva, velha* or *velhissima* ('old' and 'very old'), *5 estrelas* (five star), VSOP etc., are matured in oak for long periods. They are also caramelised as in Spain, but not overpoweringly so. Among those that I have drunk with pleasure – necessarily a random choice out of the forty that gained gold medals at the last *Concurso* – are 'Antíqua' from Caves Aliança; Delaforce Fine Brandy; Ferreira 'Reserva'; Kopke '5 Estrelas'; and 'Espirito' from J.M. Da Fonseca. Most like a French cognac in its lightness and delicacy is the 'Adega Velha' from the Quinta da Aveleda, double distilled by the Charentais method from red *vinho verde*, aged in oak and only very lightly caramelised.

Bagaceira, corresponding to the Spanish *orujo* or French *marc*, is produced all over the country in wineries large and small, from the pips and skins left over from the making of the wine. It is a water white spirit of great potency, to be sipped cautiously on pain of choking. Raymond Postgate wrote that 'it is best in my opinion not to drink *bagaceira* (or any other *marc* at all)', but I confess that I finally acquired a liking for it – it is at least *sui generis* and entirely unsweetened or artificially flavoured. One of the best, if you can find it, is the 'Cepa Velha' from Monção.

Aromatic wines and vermouths are not produced in such profusion in Portugal as in Spain. Cinzano and Martini are made by Portuguese subsidiaries and Dubonnet, under licence, by J.M. da Fonseca at Azeitão. When in Portugal it is really more sensible to drink an apéritif of the country. Dry Madeira is of course delicious, but expensive if good. Experiment with the dry white port, drunk ice-cold and much improved by a twist of lemon peel; some of the brands so-labelled are in fact semi-sweet, and it is never as dry or as fragrant as a *fino* sherry. However, you may well develop a taste for wines such as those sold by Taylors, Cockburns or Sandemans as dry or extra-dry.

11

Regional Cooking

Portugal, like Spain, has a long tradition of regional cooking; but because of its small size and the development of fast road transport, it is now possible to obtain regional specialities up and down the country, especially in Lisbon. They may best be eaten at restaurants and in the houses of friends, since the large hotels tend to serve 'international' food, while the menus at the *pousadas* and *estalagens* are as a rule ample but monotonous. When a Portuguese eats out, he expects to be served with his soup, meat (if possible steak) and vegetables, and sweet.

You should equip yourself with the red *Michelin* of Spain and Portugal and also the useful *Restaurantes de Portugal, Roteiro Gastronómico,* published yearly with the collaboration of Turismo. Turismo categorises restaurants by crossed knives and forks, displayed on a sign outside the establishment and varying from one to three; but these refer to size, décor and price rather than the quality of the cooking. It is a good idea to study the menu and the prices, usually posted outside the door. A very sensible institution is the *Menu Turistico*, which for a fixed price allows you to choose three courses *à la carte* and includes bread and butter, *vinho de casa* (house wine), service and tax.

Among the starters you should certainly try the *Caldo Verde*, the famous vegetable soup, which is made by shredding the dark green *couve* or Portuguese cabbage in a machine resembling a bacon slicer, boiling it very briefly and blending it with a purée of potato and onions, and is best supped with the dark *pão de broa* from Avintes, a bread made of rye and wheat flours. Served everywhere, it is at its best in the Minho, where it originated.

Another starter which never disappoints is the *presunto*, a ham akin to the Spanish *jamón serrano*, the best of which comes from Lamego or Chaves, near the northern border. There is in fact little to choose between the charcuterie from these places or the nearby Spanish Extremadura. With a salad, *presunto* and *chouriço* (spiced sausage) make an appetising light lunch; with the bread, which is uniformly crusty and good, and a red *vinho maduro* such as Dão or 'Serradayres', they are the makings of a picnic.

There is fish in splendid variety along the Atlantic coast and in the Algarve. Shellfish is expensive but first-rate, and when eaten cold with a mayonnaise is best accompanied by a white *vinho verde*. One or two fish dishes deserve special mention. The *Carne de Porco à Alentejana* (fried pork with clams), which originated in the south but is now served throughout Portugal, is an entirely fresh contribution to cooking; the *caldeiradas* or fish stews from the north coast yield nothing to *bouillabaisse*; and *Peixe Espada* (Scabbard fish) is grilled to perfection in the small restaurants of the Alfama in Lisbon, and is also a speciality of Madeira.

Bacalhau, a form of dried and salted cod, has been a staple commodity in Portugal (and hardly less so in Spain) for centuries. It is the national dish of Portugal, and it is said that there is a different recipe for every day in the year. It is usually served hot, but occasionally flaked and in salads. If you eat it plain boiled with potatoes, you will probably find it insipid, but there are numerous more exciting versions, such as *Bacalhau Dourado,* served with a sauce containing tomatoes, onion and garlic, or *Bacalhau Lisbonense,* which in texture resembles a creamy golden kedgeree.

The north, like Galicia, is famous for its nourishing *cozidos* or meat stews; as a foil, try a red *vinho verde*. Oporto has been famous for its tripe since the days of Prince Henry the Navigator, who sent out his ships on voyages of discovery to the African coast and Madeira. The story goes that he returned to the city of his birth in 1415 to victual an expedition against the Moors of Ceuta, salting all the available meat and leaving the inhabitants with little but the tripe for their own consumption. *Tripas à Moda do Porto,* made with haricot beans and best eaten on the spot, is a first-rate dish, whose full, spicy flavour calls for a red *vinho maduro* of character. Portions here are more than ample and menus list *doses* and half *doses*; even the smaller *dose* will probably satisfy two foreign appetites. As in Spain, one of the best of the roasts is the sucking pig (*leitão*), and if you visit Buçaco, call at Mealhada nearby, where it is still cooked in open air ovens.

The most popular sweet is the ubiquitous *Pudim Flan* (baked caramel custard); but places formerly occupied by the Moors, such as Viseu, make a wide variety of cakes and sweetmeats, which may be sampled in the *pastelarias* (afternoon tea is becoming more popular in Portugal than England!). After a week or two's sojourn, you will probably skip the sweet and ask instead for fresh oranges. They are of superb quality and the season is long, since they are grown as far north as Oporto. They are served by peeling back the skin like petals – but take care that the waiter does not heap the fruit with sugar.

Another way of finishing a meal is with the *Queijo da Serra* or *Queijo do Alentejo*, excellent semi-hard cheeses made from ewe's milk with a distinctive bite and flavour. The small cream cheeses from Azeitão are often served as an appetiser in Sebútal.

Wine Tasting

by Pamela Vandyke Price

There is nothing difficult about tasting wine, even if some people suppose it to be a mystery requiring a long initiation process! The aim of tasting is to discover an enjoyable wine, either enjoyable to drink immediately or likely to prove enjoyable after some period of maturation. When you visit a wine merchant's tasting or attend a tasting party, you are most likely to be offered samples of wines that are ready or very nearly ready to drink. When you visit a wine shipper, or anywhere in the region where wine is produced, you are more likely to get the chance of trying wines that are as yet not ready to drink. Indeed, some of the very finest wines do not make pleasant drinking at all while they are growing up and developing and there may be little temptation to swallow them. But although even a very little experience will acquaint you with different things to look out for in different wines at various stages in their development, the basic procedure of tasting is the same.

Wine is a beautiful and interesting commodity – and those who really know something about it and care for it are delighted to share their enjoyment and appreciation with even the humblest beginner as well as with the experienced. So do not be shy of trying to taste seriously. Ask questions and whenever possible try to note down your impressions of a wine *while* you are tasting it – even an hour later, your thoughts will lack precision. Also, if you remember in detail wines that you like or do not like your future shopping for wine is greatly helped. No-one wants to risk being a wine bore or wine snob, but the world of true lovers of wine is wide, hospitable and worthy of exploration.

Tasting Sense and Tasting Room Manners

The tasting room is the heart of the business of any wine establishment. Care is taken to ensure that the wines may be examined as critically as possible, and that nothing should interfere with this. It sometimes disappoints people to find that a tasting room is rather a clinical place, usually with a north light plus very strong artificial lighting, plenty of white on walls and benches against which the colours of wines may be examined, and with at least one sink and possibly several spittoons as well. But the 'picturesque' type of tasting is usually more in the nature of a party and not for the occasions when large sums of money are being allocated to the buying and selling of a firm's wines.

Visitors to the tasting room will naturally wish to conform to what may be described as 'tasting manners', by not making it difficult for anyone else to make serious use of the room either while they are there, or immediately after their visit. Scent and strongly smelling toiletries for men as well as for women should ideally be avoided or, if someone has just used scent or been on the receiving end of some pungent preparation at hairdresser or barber, it is worth mentioning the fact by way of excuse, to show that you are aware this may be a distraction. Don't start to smoke, unless specifically invited to do so, as this may make the tasting room unusable for some while, though if the occasion is not too serious the host may well offer cigarettes in his office, if not actually in the tasting room. Beware of thinking that the shallow metal or enamel cups that often stand about in tasting rooms are ashtrays – they are tasting cups, and should not be casually used!

SHARING GLASSES

At professional tastings, unless someone has a cold, mouth infection or anything that obviously necessitates them keeping a single glass for their own use, it is usual for everyone tasting to do so from a single glass, which will be standing either in front of the bottle from which the tasting sample has been drawn or on a space marked in some way on the tasting bench. Some people are hesitant about sharing a glass, but may be reminded that wine is the second oldest disinfectant in the world. If you are really disinclined to taste from a glass used by anyone else, you should make no bones about asking for one for yourself.

Obviously, a woman does not want to leave lipstick on a wine glass at any time – it looks particularly revolting – and even a slight trace can affect the taste of the wine for anyone coming afterwards in a serious appraisal of wine. But it is a very simple matter to wipe the mouth before tasting, should anyone really be at the stage when they leave traces of lipstick on every eating utensil (quite unnecessary, if lipstick is correctly chosen and applied). Men should be reminded that, if they use strongly smelling soap to wash their hands, or make use of pronouncedly fragrant aftershave lotion or any preparation for hair, they will make the glasses smell just as much as any woman's cosmetic.

A final piece of advice which may seem a little severe though is not so intended: anyone who is trying to form a precise opinion about a wine being tasted requires to be able to give that wine undivided attention. Anyone who, with a false idea of making themselves agreeable, insists on breaking in on the train of thought of the taster at such a moment, peering to see what notes have been written (the experienced taster usually evolves a shorthand which is quite indecipherable to anybody else) and generally making a noise of superficial or frivolous conversation, is likely to be more of a nuisance than a welcome guest in the tasting room. There are plenty of opportunities for asking questions and exchanging points of view without interrupting someone seriously at work, and – in case it should be thought that I am being unnecessarily stern – I must point out that some of the visitors to a tasting room may be those to whom the opportunity is both illuminating and of the greatest importance as regards their future approach to wine. To interfere with an opportunity that may come only rarely, or prevent someone from taking as much advantage as possible out of an experience of serious tasting is both selfish and boorish. The professional may be able to taste on another occasion: the visiting amateur may be deprived of a unique experience by the misplaced bonhomie of someone who really simply wants a drink and would therefore be better to cut short his visit to a tasting room and await the next stage of the proceedings outside.

SPITTING

In an age when virtually any subject can be discussed, it is astonishing that people still display hesitancy and even squeamishness about spitting out samples of wine that they are tasting. A moment's reflection will indicate that to spit out when tasting is the only sensible thing to do: not merely will the mixture of a number of different wines be confusing to the palate and probably upsetting to the stomach, but some samples may be out of condition, others, especially very young wines, undergoing some form of fermentation, and none of them may actually be enjoyable to drink. Spit them out. It is perfectly possible to eject wine from the mouth discreetly and without fuss. If you are tasting samples drawn direct from casks or vats in a cellar, it is usually acceptable to spit on the floor – remember that, if this is stone or cement, there will be some splashback, so try to avoid getting wine on your shoes or those of your companions. In the tasting room, the sink or spittoon will be sluiced down at intervals, even if there is not a tap running to keep everything fresh. Let me reiterate: spit out any samples offered for tasting, unless you are specifically given a portion of wine and advised to drink it. To swallow tasting samples risks giving yourself a stomach upset and will not improve your knowledge or experience of wine.

First Look at the Wine's Appearance

A tasting sample will only occupy a small space in the glass. Its appearance has much to reveal. Ideally, the glass should be perfectly clear and clean and on a stem, though in some regions you may have to make do with small tumblers or possibly a tasting cup of a special type.

The wine should be clear and bright, with something 'living' about it. Do not be concerned that there may be bits (known as 'flyers') in it, as these may be particles from a cask sample, which subsequent filtration may well remove. Their presence, very often, indicates a quality wine, and therefore they are not reasons for condemning the wine in any way.

Tilt the glass away from you at approximately an angle of 45° and hold it against something white, so that you can examine the colour. The living quality should be obvious, rather in the way that the water of a spring is different from the flat dull water drawn from a tap and left to stand for several days. Whether the wine is red or white, it should be pleasant, ideally beautiful to look at and give pleasure to the eye.

What the Wines Indicate by Colour

WHITE WINES

These tend to deepen in colour as they age, and, usually but by no means invariably, the sweeter wines start their life by being more golden than the pale light lemon gold of the drier wines. It is also fairly safe to generalise to the extent of saying that white wines from warm southern vineyards usually start by having a more yellow-straw colour

than those from very cold vineyards, which will be pale lemon yellow,
or almost very pale green. A really old white wine (old in terms of its
own maturity, not specifically related to its age in terms of years) may
assume almost an orange tinge, reminiscent of some of the dry
Madeiras; this, and the sort of smell and taste that can come off such
wines result in the term 'maderised' often being applied to them. It
does not mean that they are undrinkable by any means, but they will
have changed their character.

Look, too, at the actual consistency of the wine in the glass. The way
in which it clings to the sides of the glass and trails downwards with the
pull of gravity can indicate a wine of great quality if these trails (known
as 'legs') are marked. This is also indicative of the glycerine content
which will be marked in the wines that naturally contain a certain
sweetness.

RED WINES

Red wines tend to grow paler as they age, many of them being purple-
red at the outset. It is probably easier for most people to see the
different tones of colour in a red wine and it is helpful sometimes to
know that, with a very fine wine (whether you like it or not) there tend
to be far more distinct tones of colour visible as you tilt the glass than in
even a good cheap wine. Look at the 'eye' of the wine at the centre of
the liquid, and then see the gradations of colour out to the edge where
the wine meets the glass: a young red wine will be purplish down to
black, with a rim that may begin to lighten almost to a deep lilac tone.
With a little more maturity, it may become reddish and in the end a
beautiful crimson-orange with great age. Red Bordeaux probably
lightens more throughout its life than red Burgundy, which tends to be
very purple at the outset, except in certain years when the colour can
be on the light side.

Remember that, with all wines, age is relative. Some wines show
signs of great age when they are young in years, simply because they
are wines that should be at their peak while comparatively young and
fresh; others, including the very greatest red wines and certain whites,
remain apparently youthful for many years. Unfortunately, today's
economic pressures make it necessary for many wine-makers to be able
to mature their wines faster than in the past, so as not to tie up their
capital; this means that a wine which you may have heard of as taking a
long time to mature can be at its peak years before you expected this.

Caution is advisable when appraising wines solely by colour, simply
because the control of wine-making these days is a very skilled matter
and has rightly been judged as important in the appeal a wine makes to
its public. If you doubt this, get someone to prepare you two samples of
the same red wine, one of them having some additional colouring in it,
put there either with culinary colouring matter or by the addition of a
few drops of a much darker wine. You will be surprised by the way in
which you feel the darker wine to be more 'full-bodied' and possibly
'fruity'! Similarly, if you think that colour does not influence taste, try
giving a critical appraisal of a wine out of a glass that is a dark definite
colour, such as blue, green, or black: you will be astonished to find
how, once one sense used in tasting is cut off, all the others are
somehow distorted.

Smell the Wine

A wine should have a pleasant healthy smell, which, in certain wines, can be complex but which should always give enjoyment. You will release this and be able to sniff it more easily if you circulate the wine in the glass, holding the glass by the stem or, possibly, by the foot (not as difficult as it looks at the outset) and simply swinging the liquid round, putting your nose into the glass at intervals and sniffing. The aeration of the wine releases the fragrance.

Surprisingly, very few wines actually 'smell of the grape' although people often wish that they might! A few grapes, notably the Muscat, do possess a distinctive aroma, which is quite often easily identified as 'grapiness', but otherwise although certain grapes may result in wines smelling of those grapes, the associations with fruit are not always obvious. A wine should smell fresh and clean, but there are certain smells which, with young wines, may be present for a short time, indicating nothing more than that the wine is going through a phase of natural development.

These smells include the slightly beery smell which may mean the wine is still undergoing a stage of fermentation, a vaguely yeasty smell, which sometimes seems present when a wine has recently been bottled, a slightly sharp smell, often described as 'green', which may be present in even the best made wine in a year when the grapes have been unable to ripen perfectly. Or, in some instances, this green smell may mean that the vineyard contains a high proportion of young vines, the use of which is apparent in the early stages of the wine's development. Obviously woody smells can mean that the wine has been matured in new wood, this smell passing with time also, or, if the woodiness is of a soggy sort, it may mean that there is a faulty stave in the cask in which the wine has been matured.

You are unlikely to find 'corked' wine in a sample of a very young, bottled wine, but a complete absence of smell can be slightly sinister in this respect, indicating that something is preventing the wine from giving off its fragrance. It is the 'swimming bath' smell, reminiscent of chlorine, that is for me most definitely associated with corkiness – which, by the way, has nothing whatsoever to do with bits of cork being in the wine. Some people do find that corkiness reminds them of the smell of cork, but I have never been able to see this myself. A musty smell can be indicative of an ill-made wine, but it should not be confused with 'bottle stink'. This is the smell (that is often stale and flat) of the little quantity of air held in the bottle of wine under the cork, which may affect the taste of the first portion poured. A little aeration will cause this to pass very soon.

The good smells, interesting and pleasing to the nose, include a type of fruitiness, the different sorts of which will be associated with the various types of grape when the taster has gained a little experience. Young wines, especially those that are most enjoyable when drunk fairly young when they are at their peak of freshness, usually have an obvious fruity smell. Then there is a crisp almost sharp smell, like the freshness of a good apple, which can indicate the right kind of acidity balancing the fruit. This should be noticed in most young wines, especially those that are dry and light. Wines from cool vineyards tend to have more smell than wines from hot ones. The infinity of delicate, flowery, herby, and subtle depths of scent with which some of the great German and other northern vineyards are associated, and in the reds from vineyards where the vine has to struggle, such as Burgundy and Bordeaux, can be so beautiful, even while the wines are very young that, as is sometimes said, 'it is almost unnecessary to drink when the smell is so fascinating'.

With the finest wines, try to break up the general impression made on you by the smell into the first impact, anything that then reveals itself by further aeration, and finally see whether there appears to be some subtle, as yet unrevealed fragrance underneath the other smell. Wines are like people in this respect, the more obvious are not always the most rewarding. Sometimes, right at the end of a tasting, a smell can come out of a wine glass that may indicate something to look forward to in the future. Try to remain alert to register this if it is there.

Taste the Wine

Always adapt tasting techniques to what experience has taught you suits your own abilities best. But the most usual way to taste is to draw a very small quantity of wine – about a teaspoonful – into the mouth, accompanied by a small amount of air. There is no need to make a loud sucking noise while doing this, but the circumstance of pulling the wine into the mouth, plus some air, seems to sharpen up the impression it can make. Then circulate the wine in your mouth, pulling it over the tongue, letting it run along the sides of the mouth and getting a general 'feel' of what it is like: light/dry/sweetish/thick/thin/assertive/reticent/ chewy/ attaching itself to the sides of the mouth/attacking the gums (everyone's gums tend to ache after a lot of tasting!). Try to split up the numerous impressions which the wine may have to give you before you spit it out. Don't be hesitant about taking more than one sample in quick succession.

AFTER-TASTE AND FINISH

When you have tasted the wine and have spat out the sample, breathe out sharply – you will be aware of an extra smell, rather than a taste, that passes across the palate. This is the after-taste and it can reveal quite a lot about the wine: for example, it may be far more definitely fragrant than the original bouquet or smell, or it may have a lingering quality, known in wine terms as 'length', both of which can indicate that the wine has great promise and may develop considerably. Or there can be little or no after-taste, when a wine may be described as 'short'.

The way in which the wine leaves the palate is the 'finish'. Does it finish cleanly, or has it a trace of stickiness? Has it a final flourish of flavour, a definite extra touch of taste, or does it die away rapidly? The finish of any good wine, regardless of price, should be clean, and, with a fine wine, entice the drinker to take more. With a modest type of wine, the finish should at least refresh rather than cloy the palate.

THE WORK OF TASTING

Some people really do not like tasting young wines, and affirm that there is no point in doing so, as they are going to enjoy them when the wines are grown-up. This is quite true, but any musician or artist is fascinated to see someone in the same line of business rehearsing or working. The way in which wines develop is equally fascinating; and, even though no-one would claim to know exactly what a wine was going to be like at its peak, any more than even the most experienced human being could judge of the detailed progress of another human's performance, the attempt to relate experience to what a wine is saying at one time or another and the backing of one's own judgment in hazarding a view as to the evolution of a particular wine is one of the most engrossing and challenging exercises. Make no mistake, tasting is hard work. It requires great concentration and results in real exhaustion if you have subjected yourself to a long session. The fact that it is, to a wine-lover, perhaps the most exhilarating pursuit of all, is a compensation.

Remember what a particular wine has to give: a wine that should be dry ought not, in general, to lack acidity and be seemingly too sweet. A wine that is meant to develop over a period of years need not always be very amiable or even give very much impression of what it is going to be like, when it is in its early stages. A very fine wine usually makes some impression on the taster, though all wines can go through phases when they seem to smell and taste of very little. The medium priced and cheap wines are very difficult to taste: they can risk being very much alike, and experience is necessary to differentiate between their attributes and what may be their deficiencies.

Don't bother yourself with the game most wine-lovers play of getting friends to 'taste blind' until you are a little experienced. It is perfectly true that this can be great fun and teach you an enormous amount, as the stark appraisal of a wine about which you know nothing at all can be a great test of your own honesty, courage and relation of the power of your taste memory. The fact that some people, on some occasions, can identify a wide range of wines with complete accuracy, is not, by itself, a tribute to more than the luck of the day and their considerable experience; they can be equally mistaken, with reasons for being so, on other occasions. The beginner can easily be discouraged by making apparently pointless mistakes, so that it is wise not to indulge in this until you have a little general knowledge of wines.

Meanwhile, it is only sense to bear in mind that you are unlikely, for example, to be offered a range of red Bordeaux in the tasting room of a Burgundy shipper or vice versa! Nor, in one wine region, are you likely to be offered a wide range of wines from several other districts. The visitor to Bordeaux who was disappointed in not seeing where 'the sherry wines were made' is not unique! Although a firm may handle a vast range of wines, it is unlikely that the visitor will ever be asked to taste more than one type at a time. What they are offered over a hospitable table, of course, may be very much wider in scope.

Taking Notes

Notes made on the spot are far more valuable than any general impressions recorded even a short time afterwards, but it is extremely difficult to translate taste impressions into words. To put 'good' or 'bad' is really equally useless – how do you know? It may simply be that the wine in question does or does not appeal to you at that stage of your experience. Try, whenever possible, to differentiate between wines that you truly like and wines that you may admire as good but which do not particularly appeal to you. I would recommend any taster to make up his or her own set of tasting terms as far as possible. It is useless making play with technicalities only half understood from books or to use terms which may mean something to one taster but very little to another. With even slight experience, it is possible to translate your own tasting impressions into language that may be generally understood, but if it helps you, for example, to write 'carnations' or 'violets' against a particular type of wine, then do so. You associate this wine with those particular flowers and no-one else is obliged to do so. But, if, merely because someone who seems to be authoritative, insists that 'wild thyme' or 'scrubbed oak table' is inevitably associated with a particular wine, do not attempt to agree with them unless you can wholly associate yourself with the experience – it is worthless if you cannot share it, and your own impressions will be more valuable to you if you can make the effort to formulate them in terms that enable you to remember what you taste.

Always date your tasting notes and be precise about where the tasting was done, if you are not using a tasting sheet provided by the establishment. It is surprisingly easy, especially if the wines are good and seem to become better and better, for the impression at the end of any tasting to be wonderful but confused!

Deterrents to Tasting

There are a few things that make it difficult to taste. Some – smoking, scent, etc. – have been mentioned earlier. Obviously, a cold prevents you from doing so easily, and very few people find it easy to taste after they have had a large mid-day meal. The morning, when the stomach is fairly empty and both the mind and body are fresh, is probably the ideal time. Otherwise, if you wish to prepare your palate for serious tasting, remember that violently flavoured or piquant foods can make it difficult for you, and this should also be remembered when you are choosing wines to go with a meal. Of course, few people would be silly enough to eat curry, large amounts of pickles, or anything containing a high proportion of vinegar while trying to drink a fine wine, but other things can impair the receptivity of the palate, notably eggs and chocolate. Indeed, a single chocolate makes it almost impossible for me to taste for several hours afterwards! Anything very sweet, or a piece of confectionery, will also make it quite impossible to taste for some time – even a medium dry wine will taste incredibly acid after such a thing.

People are sometimes offered crusts of dry bread or biscuits to refresh the palate at a tasting, but there is one thing that you will never accept if you are being serious about the procedure – cheese. Not for nothing do the wine trade say 'we buy on apples, sell on cheese', because the alkalinity of cheese has the effect of making almost any wine taste better than it may perhaps be, whereas the acidity of an apple, or a crisp young carrot, will show up a wine quite brutally for good or bad.

APPENDIX 2

Glossary of Wine Terms

Glossary of Spanish Wine Terms

(Words and phrases commonly found on labels are listed on pp. 28–9 and 96–7)

Aguardiente. Alcohol of not more than 80° strength distilled from vegetable materials.

Amontillado. Style of sherry made by ageing the *fino* wine.

Arroba. 1. Variable liquid measure; 2. Weight of about 25 lb.

Arrope. Syrup made by evaporating down must.

Barrica. Wine cask of 225 litres capacity.

Bocoy. Large butt of variable capacity.

Bodega. 1. Wine shop; 2. Establishment where wine is made and/or blended, matured and shipped.

Bodeguero. The proprietor of a *bodega.*

Bota. 1. Small leather wine bag; 2. Butt.

Catador. Wine-taster.

Capataz. The cellarman at a *bodega.*

Cava. Cellar for making sparkling wine.

Cepa. Wine stock.

Copita. Small glass used for tasting.

Cuba. Fermenting vat.

Depósito. Large tank, usually of lined concrete, for storing or blending wine.

Fino. Pale, delicate sherry, breeding a prolific *flor.*

Flor. Film of yeast cells growing on the surface of wines of the sherry type.

Granel, a. In bulk.

Holandas. Grape spirit containing 65 per cent by volume of alcohol.

Injerto. Graft.

Manzanilla. Dry sherry made at Sanlúcar de Barrameda.

Mistela. Sweet must in which fermentation has been arrested by the addition of alcohol.

Oloroso. Dark, full-bodied sherry.

Orujo. 1. The skins and pips of the grapes removed after fermentation; 2. spirit resembling *marc.*

Pago. The area of a vineyard.

Palo cortado. Superior style of sherry, now rare; full-bodied and with a deep and aromatic bouquet.

Porrón. Drinking vessel with a long spout.

Portainjerto. Resistant stock on which the vine is grafted.

Raya. Term used in classifying musts for sherry; also used of a coarse form of *oloroso.*

Sangría. Red wine with added citrus juice.

Solera. Series of butts for maturing wine, especially sherry.

Tina. Large oak vat.

Tinaja. Large earthenware container for the making and storage of wine.

Tonel. Large storage cask containing several butts.

Tonelada. Metric ton, 1,000 kg or approximately 10 hectolitres of wine.

Tren. Bottling line.

Venencia. Small, long-handled silver cup, used for sampling sherry from the butts.

Vid. Vine.

Glossary of Portuguese Wine Terms

Adega. Cellar or winery.

Aguardente. Brandy.

Almude. Old-fashioned measure of quantity corresponding to 25 litres of wine.

Armazem. Warehouse or wine store.

Associado. Partner in a co-operative winery.

Bagaceira. *Marc,* made by distilling *bagaço.*

Bagaço. The skins and pips of the grapes removed before or after fermentation of the must.

Bardo. System of training vines on wires stretched from wooden or granite posts.

Casta. Variety of grape.

Cepa. Vine.

Cuba de Fermentação. Vat for fermenting wine.

Depósito. Large tank or vat for storing or blending wine.

Geropiga. Sweet syrup made by evaporating down must.

Hogshead. Barrel equivalent to half a pipe and containing 58 gallons or 160 litres.

Lagar. Old-fashioned stone trough used for making wine.

Lodge. One of the large wineries in Vila Nova de Gaia, where port is matured and blended.

Lote. Parcel of new wine, subsequently to be matured and blended.

Manta. The 'cap', composed of grape skins and other solid matter, which rises to the surface of the vat when making red wine.

Pipe. Barrel containing 115 gallons or 320 litres and traditionally used for port.

Quinta. Country property, sometimes an elegant house, sometimes a shed, the point being that it must include agricultural land.

Tonel. Large cask holding 13–25 pipes.

Uveira. Tree vine.

APPENDIX 3

Further Reading

Spain

Carbonell Razquín, Mateo, *Tratado de la vinicultura,* Barcelona, 1970.
Castillo, José del, *Los vinos de España,* Bilbao, 1971.
Chartreuse, S.A.E., *Chartreuse,* Tarragona, 1968.
Ford, Richard, *Gatherings from Spain,* London, 1846.
A Handbook for Travellers in Spain, London, 1847.
Gonzalez Gordon, Manuel Mª., *Sherry,* London, 1972.
Jeffs, Julian, *Sherry,* 3rd ed., London, 1982.
Marcilla Arrazola, J., *Tratado practico de viticultura y enologia españolas,* Madrid. (Vol. 1, *Viticultura,* 1963; Vol. 2, *Enologia,* 1967).
Ministerio de Agricultura, *Vides de la Rioja,* Madrid, 1965.
Anuario estadístico de la producción agricola 1974–1975, Madrid.
Reglemantacion de las denominaciones de origen de los vinos españoles (for all the regions listed in Appendix 4).
Peñin, José, *Manual de vinos españoles,* 3rd ed., Madrid, 1981.
Manual de los vinos de Rioja, Madrid, 1982.
Read, Jan, *The Wines of Spain,* London, 1982.
Pocket Guide to Spanish Wines, London, 1983.
Read, Jan, and Manjón, Maite, *Flavours of Spain,* London, 1978.
Ruiz Hernandez, Manuel, *Estudios sobre el vino de Rioja,* Haro, n.d.
Torres, Miguel A., *Wines and Vineyards of Spain,* Barcelona, 1982.

Portugal

Adega Regional de Colares, *O Vinho de Colares,* Colares, 1938.
Allen, H. Warner, *Sherry and Port,* London, 1952.
Good Wine from Portugal, revised ed., London, 1960.
Barbedo Galhano, Amândio, *Le Vin Verde,* Oporto, 1951.
Bradford, Sarah, *The Englishman's Wine – The Story of Port,* London, 1969.
Carvalho, Bento de, and Correira, Lopes, *Os vinhos de nossa pais* (English trans. *The Wines of Portugal),* Junta Nacional do Vinho, Lisbon, 1979.
Cincinnato da Costa, B.C., *O Portugal Vinicola (Le Portugale Vinicoles),* Lisbon, 1900.
Correira de Loureiro, Virgilio, *La Region Délimitée des Vins du Dão,* Viseu, 1949.
Croft-Cooke, Rupert, *Port,* London, 1957.
Madeira, London, 1961.
Howkins, Ben, *Rich, Rare and Red,* London, 1982.
Manjón, Maite, *The Home Book of Portuguese Cookery,* London, 1974.
Moreira da Fonseca, Alvaro, *O ABC da Vinificacão,* Oporto, 1960.

Postgate, Raymond, *Portuguese Wine,* London, 1969.
Read, Jan, *The Wines of Spain and Portugal,* London, 1973.
   The Wines of Portugal, London, 1982.
Robertson, George, *Port,* 2nd ed., London, 1982.
Stanislawski, Dan, *Landscapes of Bacchus,* Austin (University of Texas
   Press), 1970.

Miscellaneous

Allen, H. Warner, *A History of Wine,* London, 1951.
Blue Guide to Spain, ed. Ian Robertson, London 1975.
Blue Guide to Portugal, ed. Ian Robertson, London.
Firestone Hispania, *1:1,5000,000 mapas de carreteras* (Sheets 1–8, cover-
   ing Spain and Portugal).
Jeffs, Julian, *The Wines of Europe,* London, 1977.
Johnson, Hugh, *The World Atlas of Wine,* 2nd ed. London, 1977.
Michelin, *Red Guide to Spain and Portugal,* London.
   Green Guide to Portugal, London, 1980.
   1:1,000,000 map of Spain and Portugal.
Price, Pamela Vandyke, *A Directory of Wines and Spirits,* London, 1974.
   The Taste of Wine, London, 1975.
Redding, Cyrus, *A History and Description of Modern Wines,* 3rd ed.,
   London, 1851.
Sutcliffe, Serena, ed., *André Simon's Wines of the World,* 2nd ed.,
   London, 1981.
Vizetelly, Henry, *The Wines of the World Characterized and Classed,*
   London, 1875.

APPENDIX 4

Wine Regulations

Spanish Wine Regulations

The Government exercises overall control by means of the *Estatuto de la
Vina, del Vino y de los Alcoholes,* a decree issued by the Ministry of
Agriculture, which establishes a code of practice for all concerned with
the production and sale of alcoholic beverages. Since it runs to some
20,000 words, only the more important provisions of its seven main
títulos can be summarised.

The preamble defines the different classes of wines and spirits and as
a first requirement stipulates that wine must be made by natural and
traditional methods and normally contain not less than 9 per cent by
volume of alcohol. Limits are set for the sugar content of dry, semi-dry,
semi-sweet and sweet wines; and for the alcohol content of *vinos
generosos,* such as sherry, and for sparkling wines, vermouths and
spirits. The overriding consideration is that the drink must contain
nothing harmful to the consumer.

Título I deals with the planting and cultivation of vineyards and nurseries, which must be carried out in consultation with the Ministry and with approved varieties of vines. The use of hybrid American vines – as distinct from vines grafted on American stocks – is completely forbidden.

Título II proceeds to methods of vinification and is particularly concerned with setting limits for chemicals such as sulphur customarily used in wine-making. A series of Articles lists unacceptable defects, like bad colour or smell, bacterial and cryptogrammic infection or the presence of excessive amounts of volatile acid and directs that such inferior wines must be denatured and distilled or converted to vinegar.

The previous *títulos* establish minimum standards for Spanish wines generally; *Título III* is concerned with the quality of the wine produced in individual regions, providing that local requirements be drawn up and enforced by specified *Consejos Reguladores*. Only wine that meets these local requirements qualifies for the *Denominación de Origen* (*Appellation Contrôlée*).

Título IV regulates the distribution and sale of alcoholic beverages, empowering the Government to fix prices for certain classes of product and laying down conditions for transport and labelling. All shipments of wine abroad must be accompanied by a certificate of analysis issued by a Government laboratory.

Título V lays down heavy penalties for any establishment regarding the provisions of the *Estatuto*; while the final section charges the Ministries of Agricultura and Hacienda with drawing up a detailed register of vineyards and bodegas and proceeding with a reorganisation and extension of the *Consejos Reguladores*.

There are at the moment *Consejos Reguladores* for the following regions, shown on the map on page 6.

Alella	Navarra
Alicante	Penedès
Almansa	Priorato
Ampurdán-Costa Brava	Ribeiro
Campo de Borja	Rioja
Cariñena	Rueda
Conca de Barberá	Somontano
Huelva	Tarragona
Jerez-Xerez-Sherry	Terra Alta
Jumilla	Tierra de Barros
La Ribera del Duero	Utiel-Requena
Málaga	Valdeorras
Mancha	Valdepeñas
Manchuela	Valencia
Méntrida	Valle de Monterrey
Montilla-Moriles	Yecla

The *Reglamentaciones* issued by the different *Consejos* for the guidance of growers and bodegas within their areas are extremely detailed, each of them running to some dozens of closely printed pages. They define the boundaries of the sub-districts within the regions; specify grape types and permitted yield; and elaborate on methods of viniculture and viticulture. Tables covering different types of wine lay down limits for density, acid titre, and the percentage of dry extract and alcohol; and further sections deal with labelling, export and the maintenance of records.

Portuguese Wine Regulations

In Portugal there is a clear-cut division of responsibility between the Instituto do Vinho do Porto, dealing with port, and the Junta Nacional do Vinho, directly controlling the production of all other wines except for the *vinhos verdes* and Dão, which have their own regulatory bodies (see p. 95).

The central departments of the Junta Nacional, including accounts, finance, economic and technical research and statistics, and also the Delegação de Região Vinícola de Madeira operate from Lisbon; beyond this, the country is divided into *zonas técnicas*. Undemarcated wines, sold without a guarantee of origin, must be produced according to the general rules and specifications of the Junta Nacional. Demarcated wines must meet more specific requirements applying to the individual regions, which are:

Algarve	Carcavelos	Madeira
Bairrada	Colares	Moscatel de Setúbal
Bucelas	Dão	Vinhos Verdes

Apart from the fully demarcated regions, a Decree Law of 7 June, 1979 created a new category of 'determinate areas' supervised by the Junta Nacional and recognised by the EEC Commission as producing wines equivalent to 'Quality Wines PSR'. From north to south of the country, these are:

Douro: Alijo, Lamego, Sabrosa, Vila Real
Beira Alta: Lafões, Meda
Estremadura: Torres Vedras, Palmela
Ribatejo: Cartaxo
Alentejo: Borba, Reguengos, Vidigueira

Apart from Government control exercised through the Junta Nacional, many of the leading Madeira shippers have banded together to form the Madeira Wine Association to maintain standards and share certain production facilities. At the time of writing the member firms who ship to the United Kingdom are: Blandy's Madeiras Lda.; Cossart Gordon & Co. Ltd.; F.F. Ferraz Lda.; Freitas Martins Caldeira Lda.; Luis Gomes (Vinhos) Lda.; Leacock & Co. (Wine) Lda.; T.T.C. Lomelino Lda.; Rutherford and Miles Lda.; and Shortridge Lawton & Co. Ltd. Other well-known firms are: Adega Exportadora de Vinhos de Madeira; Vinhos Barbeito; H.M. Borges; Henriques & Henriques; Marcelo Gomes & Cia. Lda.; Sandeman Sons & Co Ltd.; and Veiga Franca & Co. Ltd.

The port shippers, who operate under the control of the Instituto do Vinho do Porto, also belong to a Gremio de Exportadores, which acts as a government-sponsored trade association, and may not export wine unless they are members. A list of some of the best-known firms appears on page 105.

Index

aguardiente (*marc*) 71, 117
Albergues 30, 31, 53, 68
Alella 5, 20–1, 55, 57–8
Algarve, the 81, 94, 95
Alicante 23, 69
Almanas 23, 133
Almendralejo 24, 66, 67
aloques 23
Amarante 89, 90, 107
amontillado 15–16, 25; characteristics 43
Ampurdán-Costa Brava 21
Andalusia 35–55, 73
anis 68–9, 71
apéritifs 71, 72, 96, 118
Aragon 24, 35, 59, 62–3, 75
arrope vinico 25, 44, 68
Association of Port Wine Shippers 82, 105
Avelada, 'green wine' 110

bagaceira 71, 96, 109, 117–18
Bairrada 80, 92–3, 95, 113; Anadia vinification plant 106, 116
Balearics 69–70
Basque region, cooking 75–6
Basto 89, 90
Benicarlo 12, 24, 60
Beronia 50
Bradford, Sarah, *The Englishman's Wine* 113
Braga 89, 90, 107
Brandy, Portuguese 96, 117
     Spanish 39, 40, 44, 68, 70–1
Buçaco 93, 115, 116, 120
Bucelas 80, 85, 92, 95, 102

Canamero 17, 30, 67
Carcavelos 80, 85, 92, 95, 101
Cariñena 24, 63
Casa do Doura 95
Castellón de la Plana 23–4, 69
Catalonia 5, 7, 20–1, 34, 35, 55–62, 75
Cenicero 47, 49
Cervanyes 68
Chacolí 24, 75
Chartreuse 34, 57, 72
Chaucer, Geoffrey 9–10

Chinchón 68–9, 71
Chiclana 37
Codorníu 34, 57, 61
Colares 80, 85, 92, 95, 102
Comissão de Viticultura da Região dos Vinhos Verdes 95, 106
Common Market 12, 20, 29, 95
Consejos Reguladores 27–8, 43; list of 133
cooking, Portuguese 76, 119–20
cooking, Spanish (regional) 73–6
cooperatives, Portuguese 62, 84, 89, 91, 109
     Spanish 19, 23, 28, 30, 34, 53, 62, 65, 66
copita 40

Dão 62, 84, 85, 90–2, 95, 110, 114–16
demarcated regions, Portuguese 80, 89, 91, listed 134
demarcated wines 92–3; regional list 134
Deonominación de Origen, Spanish 18, 19, 27, 28, 29, 44, 58, 133
dessert wines 25, 68, 88
'determinate areas' 95, 111; listed 134

El Bierzo 22
EEC 20, 29, 95, 134
exhibitions, international 29, 84
Extremadura 17, 24, 35, 66–7, 74

Factory House 103, 105, 111
Federação dos Vinicultores do Dão 90, 95, 114
Ferreira, Dona Antonio Adelaide 111–12
'ferreirinha' 111
Ferrer, José L. 70
festivals, wine 36, 47, 65, 69
Figueroa, Marqués de 65
fino, *flor* 14–17 *passim* 37, 38, 39, 40, 43
Ford, Richard 3, 11, 12, 27, 36, 38–9, 49
Forrester, J. J. (Baron) 86, 111–12
Fuenmayor 47

Galicia 5, 8, 24, 25, 35, 64–6, 71, 76, 88, 120
Greeks, in Portugal 81; in Spain 7
green wines 24–5
Guedes family 107, 110, 115

Haro 28–9, 34, 45, 49, 51, 74
holandas 70
Huelva 17, 35, 43–4

Instituto do Vinho do Porto 95, 104, 106, 134

Jeffs, Julian 21
Jerez de la Frontera 14, 15, 16, 34–9 *passim* 68, 70
    bodegas 41, 59
    wine shippers 41–2
Johnson, Hugh 3, 17
Jumilla 23
Junta Nacional do Vinho (JNV) 95–6, 102, 109, 134
    Concurso Nacional de Vinhos 96

labelling, Spanish 19–20, 26–9
    espumosos 62
lágrimas 25
lancers 93, 101
Las Campanas 62–3
Laymont and Shaw, Spanish wines 66
Léon 5, 12, 22, 55
Levante 4, 35, 67–8, 74
liqueurs, Spanish 58, 68, 72
Logroño 27–8, 34, 45, 49, 74

Madeira 27, 84, 85, 95, 116–17, 120
    history 83
    shippers 134
    'stoving' process 88, 117
    styles 88
    wine-tasting 134
Madeira Wine Association, member firms 134
Majorca 69–70
Málaga 7, 11, 12, 25, 35, 44, 73
malo-lactic fermentation 5, 63, 108
Mancha, La 4, 23, 24, 58, 133
Manchuela 23, 133
manzanillas 15, 37, 38, 42
maps for touring 34–5
Mateus *rosé* 85, 93, 106, 110
Medellín 67
Méntrida 23, 133
Mérida 66–7
Methuen Treaty 10, 65, 82, 84, 103
Ministry of Agriculture, *Estatuto* 27, 30, 132
Minorca 69–70, 73

mistela 71, 72
Monção 25, 65, 89, 107, 109
Montánchez 17, 30, 67, 74
Montilla-Moriles 14, 16–17, 35, 37, 42–4
Moors 8, 11, 35, 54, 73, 81
Moscatel de Setúbal 95
Moselles 20, 25, 90
Murríeta, Marqués de 17–19, 29, 51–2
museums, wine 32, 36, 55, 57, 59–60

Navarra 12, 20, 21, 35, 62–3
New Castile 35, 67

Olarra, new bodega 49
oidium 83
Old Castile 17, 21–2, 35, 53, 74–5
olorosos 15, 16, 37, 41
    characteristics, 43
Oporto 81, 82, 89, 103–107, 113, 120

palo cortado 15, 16, 43
paradors 30, 31, 35, 36, 53, 64
peñafiel 22, 53, 89, 90, 107
Penedès 5, 20, 59–62
Perelada 26, 55, 57, 59
phylloxera 5, 11, 22, 24, 79, 80, 83, 92
Pombal, Marqués de 82, 95, 101
porron 59
port 82–6, 103–7
    shippers 95, 105
    styles of 86–8
    vintage 82, 83, 86, 95, 104, 111, 113
Portugal, geography 79–80
    history 81–2
    wine list 96–7
Postgate, Raymond 89, 117–18
pousadas 98, 103, 108
Priorato 21, 25, 55, 57, 58–9
Puerto de Santa Marífa, wine shippers 41–2

queimada 71
quintas, port 86, 111–13

Raya 43
Redding, Cyrus 4
Regulations, Government,
    Portuguese 95–6, 134
    Spanish 18, 19, 27–9, 30, 132–3
Ribera del Duero 21, 53–4
Rioja 5, 11, 12, 17–20, 30, 34, 35, 43–53, 63, 75
    Consejo Regulador 27–8, 47, 49
Riscal, Marqués de 17, 19, 20, 22, 29, 47, 51–4

Romans 81; in Spain 7–8, 11, 42, 54, 57, 66, 67, 73
Rueda 12, 22, 53, 54

Salvatierra de los Marcos 67
San Sadurní de Noya 26, 34, 57, 59, 61, 62
sangría 58
Sanlúcar de Barrameda 15, 35, 37, 39; bodegas 42
Santiago de Compostela 25, 31, 76
Setúbal 80, 85, 92, 95
Shakespeare 10, 81, 83
sherry 4, 10–16, 70
   bodegas 34, 36, 37, 39, 60
   pagos 36–7
Sitges 25, 57, 59
soleros 15–17, 25, 38–9, 43, 44, 70
Spain, geography 3–4
sparkling wines, Portuguese 93, 113
   Spanish 20, 21, 26, 34, 51, 57, 60–1

tapas 16–17
Tarragona 11, 24–6, 34, 57, 58, 71–2
technology, and vinification 12, 61, 85
tinajas 16, 37, 44, 69, 81
Tomelloso 70, 71
Toro 5, 24, 53, 54–5
Torres 20
Torres Vedras 93, 102
Trujillo 67
Tudela 62, 63

undemarcated wines, Portuguese 85, 93–4
Upper Doura 79, 80, 85, 89, 103, 110–14
Utiel-Requena 23, 58, 68
   rosés 69

Valdepeñas 11–12, 23, 24, 35, 68, 69, 75
Valencia 23, 69, 74
Valladolid 53, 54, 74

Vega Sicilia 21–2, 29, 53–4
venencia 39–40
vermouth, Portuguese 118
   Spanish 58, 68, 71
Vila Nova de Gaia 86, 103, 111
Villafamés 60
Villafranca del Penèdés 31, 59, 60, 71
vines; Short list, Albariño 25, 90;
   Alvarelhâo 93, 110; Alvarinho
   89–90, 107, 109; Carínena 20,
   21, 61; Cayetana 24; Cencibel 23;
   Garnacho 18, 19, 20; (*blanco,
   negra, paluda, tinto*) 20, 21, 58;
   Graciano 18, 63; Lairén 23;
   Macabeo 20, 26, 58–9, 61;
   Malvasía (Malmsey) 19, 21, 25,
   59, 83, 88; Mazuelo 18, 21, 63;
   Monastrell 20, 23; Moscatel 14,
   25, 59, 60, 86, 101, 125;
   Palomino 14; Pedro Ximénes 14,
   15, 16, 25, 42, 43, 58–9;
   Tempranillo 18, 20, 21, 23, 49,
   51, 63; Touríga Nacional 85, 90,
   93, 110; Ull de Liebre 20, 21, 23;
   Viura 19, 20, 26, 61; Xarel-lo 20,
   21, 26, 61; foreign varieties 20,
   26, 60, 85, 93
vinhos verdes 5, 24–5, 62, 65–6, 76,
   79, 88–90, 95, 107–10, 120
Vínicola Navarra 21
Vínicola de Vale de Dâo 115
vino verde 24–5, 62, 65–6, 76
Viseu 114, 115, 120
visits to wineries 34–5, 40, 41, 42,
   49, 53, 63, 72, 98, 104–5
Voiron 72

wine-making, vinification process 108–9
wine tasting 121–8
wine terms, glossary 129–30

Yecla 23, 68
Ygay 49
Yoxall, Harry, *Wine and Food* 44